DOING THE WRITE THING

A Memoir

Also by Susan Berliner

GEORGE'S MOTHER AND OTHER WEIRD STORIES

SOLDIER GIRL (Book Two of The Touchers)

AFTER THE BUBBLES (Book One of The Touchers)

THE SEA CRYSTAL AND OTHER WEIRD TALES

CORSONIA

THE DISAPPEARANCE

PEACHWOOD LAKE

DUST

DOING THE WRITE THING

A Memoir

Susan Berliner

Published by SRB Books

ISBN: 978-1-7374163-0-2

Cover design by 100 Covers
Layout by Rik of Wild Seas Formatting
Author's photo by Rachel Leib Photography

Published August, 2021

Printed in the United States of America

To my husband Larry, a major part of my life

(and a major character in some of these stories)

and

In memory of Linda Commodore,

a good friend

and a devoted fan of my novels

INTRODUCTION

I never thought I'd write a memoir. I'm a writer of fiction, the author of six supernatural thrillers and two collections of weird short stories.

But I've always felt an urge to record some of the happenings in my life. Years ago, I envisioned "Growing Up 'W'" appearing in the *New York Times Magazine's* back-page "Lives" column. However, before I got around to writing that story, the *Times* eliminated its "Lives" feature. I wrote "Growing Up 'W'" anyway. And then I wrote another story, and another, and another.

I kept thinking of new true tales to write, incidents I found entertaining that I thought others (especially people who knew me) might enjoy. But since each event was short, even thirty of these stories wouldn't have been enough to fill a book.

Then I recalled a journal I'd kept as a young newspaper reporter, which I thought I had written for just a month. However, when I checked, I discovered I'd recorded the diary for eight months and even after eliminating non-relevant and repetitive entries, it still contained more than 15,000 words. Together with my short stories, that was enough for a book.

Doing the Write Thing is a collection of my memories—as true to what really happened as I can remember. I enjoyed writing the book. Hopefully, you'll enjoy reading it.

STORIES

MY WONDER YEARS

ALL GROWN UP

MY WONDER YEARS

WAR STORY

World War II was horrific, but without it my parents would never have met and I wouldn't have been born. Other than both being Austrian Jews, Olga Reitmann and Josef Wettenstein had little in common. My mother came from a well-to-do cosmopolitan Viennese family while my father's Hasidic family lived in the boondocks—a small spa town near Vienna called Baden bei Wien.

My father's mother wore a *sheitel*—the wig required for Orthodox married women—and his family employed a *Shabbos goy* (Gentile) to turn the electricity on and off during the Sabbath and religious holidays.

My mother's people were non-observant Jews. They ate pork, enjoyed Vienna's cultural activities—theater and concerts—and paid little attention to religious holidays. In fact, my mother's family didn't think of themselves as Jews.

The Nazis, however, disagreed. To them, my mother was as Jewish as my father. Although my parents fled Austria before the war began, Hitler's regime killed the members of their immediate families who remained. Those victims included my father's oldest brother and sister, their spouses and five children, as well as my parents' mothers and fathers—

all my grandparents.

My parents both escaped to England, my father first spending time in the Kitchener Refugee Camp near Kent before enlisting in the British army as an interpreter. In addition to German, he spoke English and French, having lived in Paris in his early twenties.

My mother got a job as a "domestic servant," a housekeeper for Major Sparrow, a retired and widowed army officer, who lived with his son, John, and daughter, Claire—older teenagers—and their dog, Blackie, and cat, Blackiemore, in Knutsford, a small suburb of Manchester.

It was a challenging job for my mother, who, having grown up with a maid, knew nothing about cooking and maintaining a house. But, using cookbooks, she learned to prepare meals for the Sparrows and became quite a good cook. And she enjoyed being part of the family's bustling household.

My parents met at a dance for German-speaking refugees, fell in love, and married on May 24, 1943. After their wedding, my mother remained with the Sparrows until the end of the war while my father continued his service with the British army.

Although my father was a soldier for all that time, he never excelled as a military man. In fact, he often joked about forgetting his rifle on a train in the Underground (British subway).

After the war, my parents moved to a small apartment in Sutherland Avenue near Regents Park in London, where I was born. And we lived there until we came to America in 1951.

BRONX-SITES

My parents had two good reasons for immigrating to America: First, living in post World War II London was difficult because of food rationing. In the U.S., my mother never ate margarine—only butter—after having been denied the spread for so many years. Secondly, and more important, most of my parents' relatives who escaped Austria had settled in the United States.

So in March of 1951, we cruised from the English port of Southampton to New York harbor on the ocean liner, *S.S. America*. However, because the ship had what my parents called "engine trouble," the weeklong trip took twice that time.

Since I was only four-years-old, I don't remember the voyage. But according to my mother and father, the rough ocean made nearly every passenger seasick—except me. Apparently, I loved that journey and continue to love cruising. [See "I Sailed the Ocean Blue," p. 67]

Upon arrival, we lived in a furnished Manhattan apartment for several months until my parents rented a one-bedroom fifth-floor apartment in the Bronx, across the street from the large East 180th Street subway station.

At the beginning of the twentieth century, 1186 East 180th Street had been a luxury building because of its prime location for Manhattan commuters. It featured two wide marble staircases, an elevator, and halls large enough for boys to have sports card-flipping contests and even play baseball.

However, by the time my family moved into the building, it was a glorified tenement. We had roaches, peeling paint, plus a scenic view of the apartments across from our bare concrete courtyard that probably once boasted grass, shrubbery, and flowers.

But it was home. And soon after we settled in, there was a knock on our door. "I heard you have a little girl," four-year-old Elaine said to my mother. "Can I play with her?"

That was the start of a lifelong friendship. Elaine lived with her parents, older brother, and grandmother in an apartment on my floor.

Her father owned retail businesses, first a grocery store and then a car wash, so Elaine's family didn't have much free time on weekends. But my parents did. Although both worked as clerks—my father for a small watch company and my mother for a belt factory—they were off every Saturday and Sunday and we always did something.

Because we didn't have much money, we usually got together with family or friends or went someplace free. And if we visited nearby Bronx Park, the Bronx Zoo, or the Botanical Gardens, Elaine often came with us.

———

Since my mother worked in Manhattan when most moms of young children stayed home, I needed daycare services, which were available at P.S. 67, a large elementary school on Southern Boulevard, more than a half-mile from my home. When I was old enough to attend kindergarten, I was allowed to remain at P.S. 67 so I could continue to have after-school supervision, while Elaine and the other kids in my building went to P.S. 34, the smaller, not-so-good neighborhood school.

At that time, half-day kindergarten was voluntary so I remained in fulltime nursery school until first grade. My early first-grade report card's behavior grades were marked "Needs Improvement." It took me a while to figure out that I couldn't do whatever I wanted in school, like I had in the unstructured nursery program.

I was fortunate to attend P.S. 67 because the school's innovative principal, Mr. Petluck, was affiliated with Hunter College and recruited graduating teachers. He also added new programs, including instrumental music classes for fourth and fifth grades.

Although I had no musical talent, I was placed in one of the first string instrument classes.

"Why?" my parents asked my third-grade teacher, Mrs. Levy.

"It will be a good experience for Susan," she told them.

So I learned to play the violin. Or at least I valiantly tried — and my poor parents were forced to listen to the resulting screeching sounds. Many years later, they confessed it had been difficult to smile during my futile attempts at making music.

———

Although my friend, Elaine, spent many weekends with my family, I also got to know her visiting relatives. That included Elaine's cousin, Donna, who lived in Ohio and was about a year older than us.

I didn't like Donna. She was stuck up, always boasting she was better than we were. Once when I was about eleven, she locked me in a closet, which did little to improve my opinion of her.

Donna bragged that she was going to marry a doctor and afterwards Elaine and I laughed about her foolish prediction.

But Donna got the last laugh. She did marry a doctor. In fact, she married two of them. After divorcing the first, she married a plastic surgeon who worked on her face.

"Donna looks gorgeous," Elaine told me.

I was not pleased.

_____

When I graduated from P.S. 67 after sixth grade, my parents didn't want me to attend P.S. 83, the neighborhood's middle school, so we moved to another district.

Our new apartment was in the Castle Hill Houses and it really was a new apartment because we were the first tenants in that New York City project, built for families with limited incomes.

My mother, who loved being near water, was especially excited about our fifth-floor apartment at the end of a hallway because it had a spectacular view of the Whitestone Bridge. Although we were still in the Bronx, our building was a short walk from the Long Island Sound, giving the illusion of a waterfront property. In fact, Castle Hill Beach Club and Castle Hill Day Camp were our closest neighbors.

The apartment had one other important feature: a second bedroom. In 180th Street, I had the only bedroom and my parents slept in a convertible living room couch. In Castle Hill, my parents finally had their own bedroom.

As a result of the move, I was able to attend J.H.S 127, a better school than P.S. 83. When I began seventh grade, I remember nervously standing on line, not knowing anyone. However, I made friends, many from the nearby community of Parkchester, a large private apartment complex then owned by Metropolitan Life, which was a step up from my public housing project.

_____

I had one good friend in Castle Hill. Mary lived with her parents, older brother and younger sister at the end of another of my building's fifth-floor corridors.

I still remember Mary's brother's desk because the blotter's paperweights consisted of two deer hooves—souvenirs of a hunting expedition. Although Frankie was a nice guy, those mementos always bothered me.

Mary's family was Italian and each year she and her parents invited me to help decorate their Christmas tree. They were warm, wonderful people and I enjoyed spending time with them.

Mary, who was a year older than me, was very interested in boys. She had a crush on Luis, who lived with his parents and six brothers and sisters in a ground floor unit for large families.

Mary would devise not-too-subtle ways for us to hang around Luis.

"Let's stand out by the entrance and wait for him to come out," or "He's playing basketball at the playground so let's go there," were typical suggestions.

Like me, Mary attended J.H.S. 127. But unlike me, she wasn't interested in academics. Nevertheless, we remained good friends throughout junior high school and only drifted apart in high school when she took commercial courses and I took college-preparatory classes.

———

The right wall of my Castle Hill bedroom abutted the left wall of the bedroom in the apartment across our narrow hall. When I was in high school, that bedroom belonged to Johnny, a boy my age.

Johnny attended Music & Art, a special high school for gifted kids. Unfortunately for me, Johnny's talent wasn't in art.

He was a musician who played the saxophone.

Each evening, as I sat on my bed doing homework or studying for a test, Johnny did the same. But Johnny's work was practicing the saxophone, mostly playing scales—over and over again. And since the walls between our apartments were thin, I heard every note.

What could I do? During those musical moments, I stuffed cotton in my ears and tried to concentrate on my work as best I could. The saxophone sessions finally ended when Johnny enrolled in an out-of-town college to continue his musical studies.

THE MATRONS

Calamity Jane, starring my favorite actress, Doris Day, was the featured movie on the big screen. I sat between my parents in the large theater, slouching with raised knees, munching Good & Plenty candies, and feeling quite grownup.

I was seven-years-old and this is the earliest film experience I remember. My mother and father weren't big moviegoers, mostly because movies cost money, which my family didn't have.

But on that Saturday afternoon, we walked past the cobblestoned bus hub to the RKO Chester in West Farms and sat in one of the theater's middle rows. From my seat, I had a clear view of the children whose parents had paid for their tickets, then deposited them inside the entrance, and left. Those unescorted children sat in the first two rows, supervised by matrons, a group of stern-looking middle-aged women who used their ample breasts as arm supports.

When I remember those kids, I think of orphans in a Charles Dickens novel, maybe *Oliver Twist*. That's how scared and unhappy they looked. And although the front rows aren't the best seats for viewing a movie, the kids didn't squirm. They sat silently without moving while the matrons hovered around them.

I loved *Calamity Jane* because Doris Day was the star and the songs were good. In fact, "Secret Love," became a number one hit and a signature tune for Doris.

But when I saw the film again on TV many years later, I realized the movie itself was dumb—a sharp-shooting tomboy falls in love with Wild Bill Hickok (Howard Keel) and becomes a "lady," donning a dress in the final scene.

I saw other movies during my childhood, but few at the RKO Chester. And the rare times I went there, it was always with my parents, never dropped off alone to be left to the mercy of the matrons.

TAKING A BOW

A tailor, an old lady, a fairy, a temptress, the Easter Bunny, a princess.

Those were some of the roles I played during my acting career, which spanned grades four through six.

How did I become a child actress? When I was a fourth grader—too old for after-school nursery care—I still needed supervision until my mother got home from work. I tried ballet class, but proved too clutzy to be a dancer. Then I switched to Dramatics. Since I've always loved to talk, acting was a much better fit.

Each day after dismissal, I stayed in P.S. 67 for Dramatics, run by Mr. Sweezey, a teacher from another school in our district. The name Susan wasn't theatrical enough for him so he dubbed me "Suzanne."

Much of the time, Mr. Sweezey sat in the back of the classroom, reading the newspaper, while our group of six to ten girls created various impromptu skits and tableaus. Just one boy participated, which is why I played a man, the aforementioned tailor, Mr. Stitch, in *The Fantastic Mr. C.*

———

Our one-act plays were the highlights of Dramatics. Each cast member received a professionally-printed script, mostly from Plays, Inc. (subtitled "The Drama Magazine for Young People"), and we all memorized our lines and stage instructions. We did a good job, probably because we had ample time to rehearse.

The 30-40 minute plays were performed in P.S. 67's auditorium, in conjunction with tap dance and ballet recitals, and our after-school organization, Mohegan Community Center, even charged a small admission fee—25¢ for adults and 10¢ for children.

"Poisoned the vichyssoise—how distressing!" That was my memorable line as Mrs. Ashby, the elderly houseguest in *A Case for Two Detectives*, an Agatha Christie-like murder mystery. (I still remember that line because "vichyssoise" is such an exotic word.)

After bit parts in fourth grade, I graduated to meatier roles, including Fifi LaTour, the seductress in *Abner Crane from Hayseed Lane*, who tries to rob and cheat Abner, a seemingly naive country-bumpkin.

Kathryn, a gifted young actress, played the title role of Abner. She and her cousin, Sandra, were the only two Black girls in Dramatics, and possibly in P.S. 67, which was nearly all white and Jewish.

I liked both girls and never thought much about the color of their skin. But many years later my mother told me I had been invited to a birthday party for Sandra and a group of parents had been in phone contact debating whether or not their children should attend.

My mother, who had been a victim of discrimination, was adamant about attending the party. So I went—and the party (according to my mother, since I don't remember what happened) turned out fine.

Another of my starring roles was playing the real Easter Bunny in *Bunnies and Bonnets*. I marched into the TV studio with a basket of eggs saying, "Happy Easter, everybody!"

"Sorry," Sandra, who played the receptionist, replied. "There's no call for rabbits today. The show has been cancelled."

"Cancelled?" I moaned. "But that's impossible."

My mother, an excellent seamstress, did such a good job with my bunny costume that I was a rabbit for the next two Halloweens.

———

When I was in sixth grade, my friend Rosalie and I researched kids' plays in the library near our school and found one we liked: *The King's Creampuffs*, which Mr. Sweezey agreed to produce. Rosalie wanted to be the king and I wanted the other lead role of the princess. As a result, when Mr. Sweezey auditioned me for a lesser part, I purposely did a lousy job.

But Mr. Sweezey realized what I did. Although he cast me as the princess, he chastised me for not trying my best. I've never forgotten that experience and, since then, I try to do my best at everything.

SKATING ADVENTURE

Although I've never been athletically gifted, I've always loved to ice skate. As a child, I used three New York City skating venues: Rockefeller Center, Wollman Memorial, and Kelton's.

Rockefeller Center in midtown Manhattan was small and pricey, a site that attracted tourists and rich people. Since I was neither, I skated there just once or twice.

Wollman Memorial in Central Park was the opposite of Rockefeller Center. The rink was huge and free and as a result, always crowded. When I think of Wollman's, I picture my parents' best friends' daughter, Marlene, standing on the ice with blood dripping from her fingers after a speeding skater sliced her hand.

My favorite ice skating rink was Kelton's in Riverdale. Although Riverdale is part of the Bronx, it was far from where I lived. My trip from the Castle Hill projects required either a bus and subway ride or two buses.

―――

On one winter school vacation day in the late 1950s, my cousin George and I decided to meet at Kelton's for a day of ice-skating. (I have two cousins named George, and this George is my mother's sister's son, a year older than me.) George's family lived in Washington Heights in upper Manhattan so his trip to the rink was a 15-minute subway ride.

Since all our parents worked, we had to journey to Kelton's by ourselves. But in that era, public transportation in New York City was safe for unaccompanied kids.

Kelton's was a family-owned operation with a well-maintained ice surface. Because the rink charged a small admissions fee, it was never as crowded as Wollman. And Kelton's offered two additional perks: An aroma of freshly-baked cookies wafted over skaters from the nearby Stella D'Oro factory and a small amusement park next door, called Joyland, offered rides. In fact, the park's Ferris wheel towered behind the rink.

That day couldn't have cost me much since I owned a pair of figure skates and didn't have to rent them. George and I spent money on lunch and after skating, visited Joyland to at least go up the Ferris wheel and maybe enjoy some other rides.

I don't recall what else we did that afternoon, but I definitely remember the conclusion. When I was ready to go home, I realized I had no money left, not even the necessary fifteen-cent bus fare.

George checked his wallet and discovered all he had was one subway token. Since I couldn't board a bus without money, we decided I would slip under the turnstile and go to George's family's apartment to get fare for my ride home.

So that's what we did. I rode the subway with George to Washington Heights and he gave me the fare money. Instead of taking two buses for the return trip, I took the train to Castle Hill Avenue and then hopped on the #13 bus.

In retrospect I wonder why we didn't ask someone at the skating rink for the bus fare since I needed just fifteen cents. But if we had, I wouldn't have had such a memorable adventure.

THE *GOYISHER* TABLE

When I was fourteen, my parents and I were invited to the bar mitzvah celebration of my father's cousin's son.

"She was born a Wettenstein," my father told my mother and me, as if the fact that his cousin had shared our last name was reason enough to journey to Brooklyn to honor a boy none of us had ever met.

But attending the event was important to my father, who had lost so many relatives in the Holocaust. Also, my father's surviving close family—his brother, two sisters, and their spouses—was going. So on the designated Sunday, we set out for the far-away borough of Brooklyn.

Because we lived in the Bronx and didn't own a car (my parents never learned how to drive), for us a trip to Brooklyn was like traveling to a foreign country. Although we visited friends and relatives in Manhattan and Queens, we never ventured into Brooklyn. But that day, after taking a bus and a couple of subway trains—a trek of nearly two hours—my parents and I arrived at the bar mitzvah venue.

In the lobby, my parents attempted to greet my father's cousin and her husband. But the bar mitzvah boy's father refused to acknowledge my mother. He wouldn't look at her or even shake her hand. This weird-looking man—with a long black beard and ringlets running past his ears, dressed in black and wearing a tall black hat—turned away from my mother, completely ignoring her.

My mother, normally a placid and friendly woman, was furious. Although my father was embarrassed, there was nothing he could do. While he and his immediate family were no longer religious Jews, his cousin had married a Hasidic man and remained observant.

As my parents left the lobby to find my uncles and aunts, I stayed near the entrance. Since my two cousins hadn't accompanied their parents (who maybe realized the situation), I didn't know any of the kids. Also, I wanted to examine these strange people, having never been among Hasidic Jews.

While I studied my surroundings, a big burly guy wearing a yarmulke and sporting a bushy red beard, burst into the vestibule muttering to himself in Yiddish. Since my parents spoke German, I understood Yiddish. The man, who I later discovered was the event manager, ignored me as he continued to mumble.

"What am I going to do?" he complained. "They refuse to sit apart. They insist on sitting together. *A goyisher tish.* What can I do?" He continued whining for several minutes, repeating the words, "*goyisher tish.*"

Although I understood the language, I had no idea what the man was talking about.

A few minutes later, all the guests were called into the banquet room and directed to assigned tables. I joined a table of girls on one side of the room, which had tables of only females. The other half of the room had tables filled with just men and boys.

But in the middle of the room—between the men's and the women's sides—stood one table. Four men and four women sat there: my mother and father, my three uncles, and my three aunts. The *goyisher tish*.

———

The following year, we were again invited to Brooklyn for the bar mitzvah celebration of my father's cousin's younger son. This time, my parents, as well as my uncles and aunts, declined the invitation.

CAMP DAYS (AND NIGHTS)

Since both my parents worked, I went to day camps every summer. But when I was thirteen, I tried sleepaway camp for the first time—and loved it. For two years, I attended Camp Ella Fohs in New Milford, Connecticut, operated by the Federation of Jewish Philanthropies (meaning the camp was subsidized and my parents could afford the cost).

The next summer, however, I reached that in-between age: too old to be an Ella Fohs camper and too young to be a counselor. When my parents searched for an inexpensive camp that accepted 15-year-old campers, they found Mikan, a Federation camp run by the Henry Street Settlement on Manhattan's lower east side.

"Rustic" is a polite one-word description of Mikan. The camp was located in New York's Harriman State Park, which didn't allow toilets. As a result, our bathroom facilities were latrines: long wooden strips with cutout oval holes. Besides being disgustingly smelly, latrines posed two dangers: rear-end splinters and the dreaded case of latrine rash.

I started the summer in Bunk 5R, the cabin with the oldest campers. Some of my bunkmates were a bit weird and two were developmentally disabled. But I made one good friend,

Natalie, from Brooklyn, and we had a great time together.

Our counselor, Alice, was just 16-years-old. But she was a cool and popular girl, much more sophisticated than me.

Most of my bunkmates attended camp for just the first "trip" (three-weeks), while I was signed up for the entire three-trip, nine-week summer. Because I was considered a good camper, after the second trip I was "promoted" to the Training Unit, the bunk for potential counselors.

The girls there were a mixed bag: poor kids from the lower east side, the Bronx, and Brooklyn, along with affluent Long Islanders. Bonnie, my best friend in the Training Unit, was another Bronxite, a fellow only child, who lived with her divorced (a rarity then) mother.

———

The following summer, I returned to Camp Mikan as a Junior Counselor. My first assignment was in Intermediate Camp with six 12-year-old girls, all good friends from the lower east side.

The girls were delightful kids who enjoyed camp activities and were fun to be with. But Karen, the Assistant Counselor (Ass) who was my superior and shared bunk duties with me, wasn't much fun. She preferred to sleep all day. So while she slept, I hung out with the girls.

My most memorable experience of that three-week trip was the "social" (dance) arranged for our girls and the corresponding bunk of 12-year-old boys in Camp Recro, our brother camp next door. The girls were excited about dressing up, putting on makeup, and traveling to boys' camp for their special evening.

However, as we approached Recro's social hall—before the girls even entered the building—all the boys jumped out the windows and ran away. Of course the windows were on the ground level, but the boys really did jump through them. And they didn't return. Although my campers were devastated, they learned an important lesson: Twelve-year-old boys do not like dancing with girls.

My assignment for the second trip was in the tents. This was the oldest Intermediate Camp division and housed 13-year-old girls. But even by Mikan's standards, the tents' accommodations were poor.

While the camp's cabins weren't fancy, they were at least solid buildings that contained roofs, beds, and cubbies for storing clothes. The tents were bare raised wooden platforms with a center pole to hold the heavy canvas that was attached each summer.

And the cabins had doors. The tents had flaps that didn't close well. We couldn't even unpack our clothes because the tents had no cubbies. Moreover, we needed lanterns at night since the tents had no electricity.

There were two small tents for two. I shared the first with Joanne, a fellow Junior Counselor who had been with me in the Training Unit. Since Joanne was another popular, sophisticated girl, the two of us had little in common. Also, Joanne had gone to Camp Mikan her entire life—her brother worked in the kitchen and her mother in the office. In addition, Joanne and my best camp friend, Bonnie (a waitress that summer), were archrivals. Despite all this, she and I coexisted well.

The other small tent behind us housed two campers, Rona and Sharon. Rona was a beautiful, sweet girl who became a registered nurse. I know this because, about ten years later, her face was plastered all over the New York metropolitan area in ads promoting the nursing profession.

Further down the path, a main tent housed eight campers and our General (head) Counselor, Bobbie.

The tents were okay on clear days, but wet weather posed problems. Light rain created mildew and mustiness. Heavy rain was worse because it flooded the small tents.

During one torrential nighttime storm, Joanne and I, plus Rona and Sharon, evacuated our quarters and fled to the big tent. That night the four of us slept with the main tent's occupants and somehow I ended up sharing Bobbie's bed. Our General Counselor was a terrific person—but she was also very large, weighing over two hundred pounds. I scrunched in her bed, trying to sleep while listening to the raccoons outside knock over our garbage cans.

For the last trip that summer, I supervised nine-year-old campers in Junior Camp, which made me realize I preferred working with older girls. The campers were whiny and needy, but the Ass, another Susan, was fine. Although our cabin wasn't the greatest because it was on top of a steep hill, at least it was an enclosed building with cubbies and doors.

———

All Camp Mikan counselors received several days off during the summer. My main objective on those days was to get out of camp and go somewhere else—anywhere. But doing that wasn't easy because few counselors were old enough to drive and even fewer had cars at camp.

The only way I could escape camp on my days off was to hitchhike. Fortunately, although our camp was secluded, the road outside led to Harriman State Park's public recreational areas, like Lake Tiorati, so many cars passed by. And I always hitchhiked with another female counselor.

Several times I hitched to nearby Bear Mountain and enjoyed an afternoon there, reveling in being able to flush the toilet.

One day, I hitched to the city of Newburgh and saw an x-rated movie: *Lolita*. Another time, my companion and I were picked up by a policeman in an unmarked truck and were terrified he'd arrest us. But the officer understood our dilemma and only warned us to be careful when hitchhiking.

However, my most memorable day off didn't involve any hitchhiking. While nearly all counselors were either poor or barely middle-class, I discovered one who was both rich and well-connected.

Until Anne confided in me, I didn't know her mother was on the board of the Federation of Jewish Philanthropies or that she attended Dalton, a private Manhattan school. And one of her classmates was the grandson of former New York governor, Averell Harriman, whose family had donated the 47,000 acres of land comprising the state park that housed our camp.

Since the Harrimans still owned property nearby, Anne's classmate had invited her—and her friends—to visit his mother. Although I hardly knew Anne, who was quiet and unassuming, she and I had the same day off, as did a waterfront counselor, also named Sue, and Anne asked both of us to join her.

On that sunny day, a car pulled into camp and the driver took us to the cottage where Harriman's daughter, Mary Fisk, was spending the summer. Although her son wasn't there, Mrs. Fisk knew Anne and welcomed us. Then, after the driver loaded a huge picnic lunch into the car, he transported the three of us to the Harriman family's private island.

It was a magical afternoon. We ate a delicious lunch and skinny-dipped in a crystal-clear lake—unlike Camp Mikan's murky Lake Cohasset—with nothing but fish watching us. I remember thinking, *So this is how rich people live...*and I've never forgotten.

GROWING UP "W"

Because my maiden name, Wettenstein, is so long and uncommon, people tended to mispronounce and misspell it. But that was just a minor problem. The major problem I had with my maiden name was its location—at the end of the alphabet.

In school, most things were done alphabetically and as a "W," I was always at the rear of the line, waiting longer for everything from project assignments to team sign-ups.

In many junior and senior high school classes, teachers relegated me to the back of the room. As a result, I had lots of "W" friends. I remember sitting in the last row in French class at James Monroe High School, between Weiss and Wolf. But that wasn't so terrible; at least I had a seat.

In honors American History, we had more students than desks. The teacher's solution? After seating the class alphabetically (of course), he then directed me and the other two remaining "Ws" to the back (where else?) of the final row. So for an entire semester, I shared a small attached seat and desk with a fellow "W."

The alphabet problem didn't improve when I entered Queens College, part of the City University of New York

(CUNY). Incoming freshmen registered last and the new class was divided the usual way: Students with last names A-K went first, followed by L-Z.

My first college registration was done in person at the school. Each table offered a different course and students moved from table to table, signing up for classes. I had no trouble getting enough required 3-credit and 4-credit courses (Calculus, Western Civilization, Prose Fiction, Intermediate German) and I also managed to add a 1-credit course (Appreciation of Music).

That gave me 14 credits. But I still needed another 1-credit elective. However, since I was among the last group of registering students, the 1-credit elective courses that didn't require pre-requisites were all filled and closed. If I took just 14 credits, I'd have to go to summer school. The situation seemed hopeless...

But then I got lucky. My best friend, Barbara—also an incoming "W" freshman—had an older brother, Irving, a senior at Queens College, who had concocted a plan.

When Irving registered, he had signed up for several 1-credit electives he didn't need. At our registration, he met Barbara and walked to the elective-course tables with his sister, dropping the now closed classes, which she immediately picked up.

And Irving had taken an elective Barbara didn't want. So I accompanied him to the Health Education table where he dropped the 1-credit Hygiene course and I grabbed it.

During that first semester, when the Hygiene professor took attendance of the thirty-student class, the name he called before mine started with "K." I snickered silently each time, but I don't know if he ever wondered how a "W" snuck into his course.

By the following spring, computerized registration allowed students to select classes from home so the process was much easier. Also, I was no longer an incoming freshman.

And by the time I graduated from Queens College, I'd found an easy solution for my alphabetical problems: I married a "B."

RIDES WITH SHERRI

I commuted to Queens College from the Bronx each weekday morning, taking the #13 bus from my apartment in the Castle Hill projects to Bruckner Boulevard and then waiting in front of the White Castle restaurant for the #Q44 bus that traveled over the Whitestone Bridge into the borough of Queens.

Many mornings, several Q44s would whiz by without stopping, packed with teen girls in kelly green uniforms—St. Helena's High School students—whose school stood at the edge of the Bronx.

One day early in my first semester, after the crowd of green exited and the Q44 was relatively empty, I noticed a girl my age with Queens College notebooks on her lap sitting by herself. I smiled at her and we started talking.

Although Sherri lived in Parkchester, near my former junior high school, I'd never seen her before because she hadn't attended local schools. Since her father was an Orthodox rabbi, she had studied at Ramaz, a small progressive Manhattan yeshiva.

To Sherri, Queens College, a school of about 15,000 students, was overwhelmingly large. The size of the college had never bothered me because I'd always gone to large public schools. My high school, for example, had more than 4,000 kids.

Interestingly, Sherri's best friend at Queens College was Elizabeth, a devout Catholic girl, because the two of them had something in common: They both came from small religious schools and felt uncomfortable in our big secular college.

After that first morning, Sherri and I met on the Q44 bus many times. Although she was Orthodox, Sherri was unlike the Hasidic Jews in my father's family. She dressed like I did, wore makeup, and was smart and funny.

But she was different. Sherri didn't eat any food in the college cafeteria and to observe the Sabbath, had to be home before dark on Fridays. One Friday, she left college late, got off the bus before sundown, and walked the rest of the way—a distance of several miles.

Sherri and I were friends throughout college and even attended each other's wedding. Her wedding was memorable—not because of the religious aspect—but because of the spectacular entertainment.

Sherri married her sister's husband's younger brother and both men came from a family of cantors, religious leaders who accompany the rabbi in prayer-related songs. At Sherri's wedding reception, all five brothers performed a musical medley, singing a mixture of Jewish songs and popular show tunes. It was like attending a Broadway show.

I lost touch with Sherri soon after her wedding. I do know she became an elementary school teacher, had a child, and later divorced her husband. But we didn't have enough in common to maintain our friendship.

JODI LOVES ALAN?

In the City University of New York schools, in addition to sororities and fraternities, we had houseplans—social organizations for poor folks, with no pledging or heavy expenses—formed for the sole purpose of guys meeting girls or girls meeting guys. When I was a Queens College freshman, I joined Harmony House and received a cute music-note pin, which I still have.

Jodi was a sophomore member of Harmony House and since we belonged to the same houseplan, the two of us sat together when we took the same class that spring. I don't remember the course, but I do remember that Jodi spent the entire semester writing her name and her fiancé's name over and over in loopy letters in her QC notebook. "Jodi & Alan," "Jodi Loves Alan," "Alan Loves Jodi," often inside hearts, covered many pages.

She also flashed her huge pear-shaped diamond engagement ring and showed me photos of the wonderful Alan.

After the course ended, I didn't see much of Jodi. We were acquaintances rather than friends and since she was engaged, Jodi didn't attend our Friday or Saturday night houseplan parties. By the time I graduated from college, I had lost contact with her.

A few years later, I celebrated New Year's Eve with my husband, Larry, and another couple at a fancy Long Island restaurant. As I glanced at the other diners, I noticed Jodi, sitting at a table for two. But the man next to her wasn't Alan. And Jodi wasn't wearing her glitzy engagement ring.

I smiled at Jodi and she recognized me, but then looked embarrassed and quickly turned away. So although the question, *What happened with Alan?* bothered me that entire evening—and I annoyed my tablemates about it—I forced myself not to confront Jodi.

After the holiday, however, I played detective. Like me, Jodi had majored in elementary education so I phoned my good friend, Rhoda, also a Harmony House member and teacher, who knew someone who worked with Jodi, and asked Rhoda to uncover the story.

This is what she found out:

Alan had been unfaithful to Jodi, but not with another woman. The culprit was a horse. Without asking or telling Jodi, Alan had purchased a racehorse.

Owning a racehorse isn't like having a pet dog or cat. Besides food, racehorses require housing, trainers, and trailers for transportation—needs that cost a lot of money—and Alan had used all the couple's savings to pay for his horse's necessities. When Jodi discovered the missing money, she confronted Alan, and then divorced him.

That spiral notebook filled with their names inside hearts? What a waste of time!

ALL GROWN UP

WHEN SUSAN MET HARRIET

"Do you really have to go out tonight?" my mother asked. "The weather is terrible."

I looked at the drenching rain pelting the window and nodded my head. "Yes," I said. "I have to go."

It was Friday night in late September of 1965 and I was a sophomore at Queens College. All Bronx members of Harmony House had been campaigning for a houseplan party in our borough, instead of in Queens, and it was finally happening.

And not only was that night's party in the Bronx, it was with Compton, a City College houseplan of graduate students—"older" guys. So I stood in the pouring rain waiting for the #13 bus to take me to Parkchester to meet my friends, including Dee, who I hadn't seen since high school.

From Parkchester, Barbara drove the four of us (Dee, Rhoda, and me) to the party, held in the basement (which Compton rented) of a small brick row home on Morrison Avenue, near our alma mater, James Monroe High School.

After taking off my wet raincoat, I started talking to two guys in the vestibule who jokingly pretended to have girls' names. I don't remember the name Van used, but the cute and funny redhead who took my phone number told me his name was "Harriet."

I spent the rest of that night mostly interacting with my Bronx friends and listening to Dee, who had a beautiful voice, sing and play the guitar. There wasn't much dancing or food.

I later learned that Compton was disbanding, ending its lease, and our Friday night party was the houseplan's last. In fact, Larry (aka "Harriet") only attended the party to pick up a trophy. Even though he wasn't a star player, Larry did take home a football trophy, which is now displayed in our den.

At that time, Larry wasn't looking for a date because he was seeing two other girls, something social rules then allowed unless you were "going steady." Despite taking my number, Larry had no intention of calling me. However, when both girls turned him down for a date for the following Saturday night, I became option number three.

I agreed to go out with him, but couldn't recall his name. We hadn't talked to each other much, and I only remembered "Harriet."

On our first date, we saw *Von Ryan's Express*, starring Frank Sinatra, at the Globe movie theater in Pelham Parkway, where Larry and his family lived. Afterwards, we went out to eat and I just ordered jello because I'd already eaten dinner, impressing him as a cheap date.

Both girls Larry had been seeing called him during the following weeks. But he never went out with either of them again. We got engaged in 1966, married in December of my senior year in college, and have lived happily ever after for more than fifty years.

THE DATING GAME

"Susan Wettenstein?"

It was just my second date with Larry, doubling with one of his best friends, and I knew the girl in Bruce's car.

"Arlene Friedman?" I responded. We had gone to high school together. Arlene had been in both my tenth-grade English class and small senior homeroom when she was vice-president of the January graduating class and I was a yearbook editor.

In retrospect, I shouldn't have been surprised to know Larry's friends' dates since Larry and most of his friends had attended James Monroe High School too. Because his friends were several years older than me, I knew their younger siblings, or in this case, girlfriend.

After a tumultuous on-and-off relationship during which Bruce dated nearly every girl I knew, he and Arlene married, moved to Rockland County, and we stayed close friends until several years ago when they relocated to California.

———

Two of Larry's best friends had gotten married the summer before he and I met and our third date was with one of these couples. Since none of my friends were married, I was intimidated by going out with such grown-up people.

On that Saturday night, we went bowling with Lenny and Lori, who I really liked. Nevertheless, I was still awed by the fact that they were married.

After we bowled our games, Larry and Lenny decided it would be fun to have a contest: They would both throw a ball down the lane at the same time to see which ball would get there first. Although Lori and I tried to talk them out of their little competition, they didn't listen to us and did it anyway.

Unfortunately, when the first ball hit the pins, the metal gate automatically lowered, not allowing the second ball to reach the pins. Instead, that ball smashed hard against the heavy steel contraption.

The manager was furious at Larry and Lenny and threw the four of us out of the bowling alley. So much for Larry's "mature" married friends.

Despite that incident, we've remained close friends with Lenny and Lori and have gone to many places together—but never again to a bowling alley.

WHAT'S IN A NAME?

Wettenstein was a difficult surname for my father to deal with, but he also had a problem with his first name. It was Josef and nearly everyone in the United States spelled it with a "ph," making it Joseph.

After years of correcting the spelling of his first name, my father finally gave up and had his name legally changed to Joseph.

Not long afterwards, I met Larry, whose father had been born in America. And what was Larry's father's name? It was Josef.

My father laughed about the ironic situation, especially when he read our printed wedding invitation: "Mr. and Mrs. Joseph Wettenstein and Mr. and Mrs. Josef Berliner are happy to announce the marriage of their children, Susan and Larry..."

"THE HOUSE FOR YOU!"

"Your realtor called and said she's found the house for you!"

I discovered the above note on my desk in the early afternoon of December 28, 1971 after returning to the office from a retailing assignment for *Daily News Record* (*DNR*).

Larry and I had decided to move from our one-bedroom Flushing, Queens apartment to a single-family house in the suburbs and on Halloween we'd fallen in love with the northern Westchester town of Yorktown. (The gorgeous fall foliage helped.)

However, despite checking homes for sale in Yorktown each weekend, we hadn't seen anything we liked in our price range. We would have purchased a splanch (split ranch) near the Taconic Parkway, but it cost $45,000, more than we could afford.

Now, however, our realtor claimed to have found "the house" and when I phoned Ruth, she was excited. This listing had just come on the market and she insisted we see it that night, even though the holiday period between Christmas and New Year's Day is considered the slowest time for home sales.

"It's underpriced at $41,000 so I'm afraid someone else will grab it," she explained.

Since Larry was a teacher, he was on vacation for the week and had driven to Pelham Parkway in the Bronx, near his parents' home, that Tuesday to play handball with a friend. I planned to meet him at his family's apartment for dinner so I called Larry's mother to leave him a message about the house.

"Larry's here," his mother said.

After she put him on the phone, I excitedly recounted what the real estate agent told me. "And Ruth insists we check it out tonight," I added.

When Larry didn't respond, I finally realized something was wrong. "Why are you at your parents' apartment?" I asked. "You're supposed to be playing handball."

Larry told me he had been playing handball—until he lunged for a ball, missed it, and separated his right shoulder. He'd already been to the local hospital where a doctor yanked his arm into place, bandaged it with yards of yellow cloth, and gave him painkillers.

"I can look at the house," he said, slurring his words. "But I can't drive."

At that time, I didn't know how to drive and neither of Larry's parents had a driver's license. But fortunately we did have an alternative driver: Larry's younger brother, Howard, who lived with his mother and father.

So after dinner that evening, Howard drove all of us—including my in-laws—forty miles north to Yorktown to see the house.

The first thing I noticed when we reached the split-level home was a huge airplane mural nailed onto the siding between four front windows. And if that wasn't enough of an aviation motif, a large airplane mobile greeted us in the entranceway—along with two huge German shepherds that lunged for Larry's crotch.

Not surprisingly, Bob, the owner of the house, was a pilot for Eastern Airlines, a man undoubtedly proud of his profession.

The house was uncomfortably hot, perhaps 80 degrees, and it was poorly decorated. Ugly gold tufted carpeting, installed by the builder in the mid-1960s, lined the hallway and from there visitors were treated to a view of the living room couch's protruding stuffing.

The kitchen was painted turquoise, equipped with appliances the same color, and a huge crossword puzzle decorated the rear wall.

But although the home was unloved, it wasn't dirty because the family employed a weekly cleaning woman.

We bought the house that night and still live there. The airplane decor is long gone, along with the gold carpet (except for a small patch that no guests see, which covers the floor of the master bedroom closet). The kitchen is now brightly wallpapered and the appliances are bisque (formerly known as beige) and stainless steel.

But most importantly, the house is loved.

CHEAP! CHEAP! CHEAP!

My Aunt Malvin and Uncle Gusti invented regifting. They distributed the presents they received to other individuals long before the concept became popular. In fact, my father's older sister and her husband were the cheapest people I've ever met.

I knew Malvin and Gusti well because after coming to the U.S. from Israel in the early 1950s, they moved into a second-floor apartment in my 180th Street building. And since my parents didn't own a television set, I watched "The Wonderful World of Disney" on their TV each Sunday evening. (In retrospect, it's surprising they had a television. Maybe their TV was one present they didn't regift.)

My apartment wasn't luxurious, but Malvin and Gusti's home was the pits. Their living room window had a scenic view of the subway station's platform, enabling them to see passengers' legs and hear the booming rumble of trains entering and leaving the station. I always wondered how my aunt and uncle managed to sleep at night.

———

When Malvin and Gusti returned to Austria, which they did frequently, they never booked a hotel. They either stayed at the homes of people they knew or lived in hostels—places mostly associated with backpacking students that offered cheap housing with just the bare necessities: dormitory-style cots, thin blankets, and communal bathrooms.

And my aunt and uncle weren't young at the time; they were in their sixties and seventies.

It's not that Malvin and Gusti couldn't afford better accommodations. They could. They just didn't want to spend their money.

———

When my parents and I moved to Castle Hill in the late 1950s, Aunt Malvin and Uncle Gusti relocated to another Bronx housing project. I remember visiting them there and eating greasy apple strudel while sitting next to their continuously molting parakeet that cursed in German.

Then in the early 1970s, Malvin and Gusti followed my mother and father to a new public housing development in Far Rockaway, Queens—facing the ocean—again living in the same apartment building.

One day, Larry and I had lunch with my parents and Malvin and Gusti at a local coffee shop. During the meal, Uncle Gusti took out a small notebook filled with mathematical calculations, smiling as he showed it to us.

"I check all the supermarkets and if one store has what I want for a nickel less, I go there," Gusti said, explaining that he kept a record of every cent he'd ever spent.

Cheap! Cheap! Cheap!

PET PARADE

My first pet was a turtle with a death wish. When I was 6- or 7-years-old and my parents and I took our annual two-week vacation to Livingston Manor in the Catskills in early July, we brought the turtle to the apartment of friends. Unfortunately, they placed the turtle's bowl near an open window and my pet climbed out.

After that experience, I graduated to parakeets. My most memorable bird was Chirpy, who would repeat his name and fly onto my finger.

Since Larry also had pet parakeets as a child, after we married and moved into our Flushing apartment, we bought a bird. But Hercules was misnamed: He was a coward. Whenever one of us approached, he ran from a perch to hide on the floor of his cage.

After we relocated to Yorktown, we put Hercules' cage in the den, hoping a quiet room would improve the bird's temperament. Unfortunately, however, Hercules continued his fearful behavior.

One day, the toddler daughter of visiting friends scratched her chest on our swing. Trying to cheer up the crying child, the girl's mother took her to the den to visit Hercules.

"Look at the birdie," she said, peering inside the cage. As usual, Hercules was on the floor. But this time, the parakeet was dead.

_____

Larry and I also had pet tropical fish. They were beautiful, but not much fun to play with. Then, when our children—Meredith (Merri) and David—were young, a teacher friend of Larry's gave us a guinea pig that we named Bunker.

I was happy because, as a child, I'd always wanted a guinea pig. But my mother refused to get one. "They smell, don't do anything but eat, and the cage needs to be cleaned all the time," she explained.

My mother was right. Bunker ate pellets, squeaked (at the sight of food), slept, and pooped. His cage did stink and had to be frequently cleaned. Although we tried to find guinea pig toys, there were none—just food treats. Bunker was a big furry blob that purred when petted. But our family loved him.

_____

When Merri and David were older, they both wanted pets of their own. Since guinea pigs were big and smelly, we opted for a smaller rodent: the hamster.

After naming her first hamster, Squeaky, Merri gave all subsequent pets nutty names—Peanut, Pistachio, Almond, Walnut, Cashew, and Macadamia.

My daughter had a small pegboard rack for hanging clothes next to the hamster's cage. One day, she decided to wear a gray and white knit shirt that she'd left hanging there. However, when she removed her shirt from the peg, she discovered the hamster had unwoven an entire sleeve and repurposed it for bedding.

Merri continued to have pet hamsters even after getting married. I thought of her as the Hamster Whisperer because she could do everything one-handed while a hamster slept contentedly in her other hand.

———

David chose a combination of weird and ordinary names for his hamsters: Moley, Ohh, Charles, George, and Mr. Cool. One Saturday morning, David, Larry, and I were at the library after David's basketball or soccer game when we got an urgent phone call from my daughter.

"Moley just had babies!" Merri told us.

We rushed home and tried to separate the children from their cannibal mother before she ate them all. We were successful in saving Ohh, who we kept in a separate cage until he was old enough to be reunited with Moley without being her lunch.

Mr. Cool, another of David's pets, was memorable for his remarkable talent: That hamster was an excellent sports prognosticator. On a sheet of paper listing professional football games, David would place a seed next to the names of each of two competing teams. Whichever seed the hamster ate first determined the winner—and Mr. Cool was much better at picking winning teams than any of us humans.

UNCLE MURRY'S FUNERAL

Uncle Murry, Larry's mother's sister's husband, was a big guy with a gruff voice. As a kid, Larry had been scared of the man. Murry's gravely speech was probably due to a lifetime of smoking cigarettes and the resulting emphysema ultimately led to his death in June of 1990.

The funeral service was held in Murry's home borough, Brooklyn, far from our house in northern Westchester. But Uncle Murry was a close relative so Larry and I made the trek. And for the first time, we took our teenage children with us to a funeral because they too had known the man.

After a short service, all the cars lined up in the funeral parlor's parking lot to follow the hearse to the cemetery, many miles away in Long Island. We didn't receive any written instructions. Maybe we were told to take the Long Island Expressway to Exit 49, but not much else.

Larry maneuvered our car near the end of the line, blinker lights on, and made a right turn into busy Kings Highway. When the traffic signal changed to red, we watched the funeral procession continue ahead without us.

In those pre-cellphone days, we had no way of communicating with anyone involved in the funeral so we continued driving through Brooklyn to the Long Island Expressway. We soon encountered two other cars from our family that had also been left behind at the red light: Larry's brother and wife with Larry's mother in one car and his uncle (Larry's mother's brother) with his two adult children in the other. We waved to our relatives and stayed together until somewhere on the Expressway we caught up to a procession of blinking lights.

Smiling to each other from car to car about our good fortune, our mini-motorcade joined the end of the funeral line, continued driving to Exit 49, and turned into the cemetery. Then all the mourners got out of their cars and gathered around the open grave.

The ten members of our family stood there for several minutes, looking at the other people. *Where was Aunt Anne— Uncle Murry's widow? Cousin Iris—Uncle Murry's daughter? Ivan, his son?*

At about the same time, the realization hit each of us: They weren't there. We were at the wrong funeral.

We ran to our cars and drove into the adjacent cemetery. When we entered the office, Iris was finishing the paperwork for her father's burial. But the funeral was over. We had missed it.

We explained what had happened and Iris was very understanding. In any case, there was nothing she or we could do. So the first burial my children attended was for someone we didn't know.

In the years since, we've been to other funerals in that confusing line of adjoining cemeteries off Exit 49 of the Long Island Expressway. But thanks to modern technology, we've always been able to arrive at the correct gravesite.

I SAILED THE OCEAN BLUE

I've loved ocean voyages since coming to America as a young child on the *S.S. America*. Therefore, it's no surprise that my favorite vacation is a sea cruise.

Because I was one of the few passengers who didn't get queasy on the lengthy journey across the Atlantic, I thought I'd never get seasick on a boat. However, on a mid-1980s cruise to Mexico, traveling from Playa del Carmen to Tulum to tour Mayan ruins, I noticed brown bags hanging above the planked seats of our giant catamaran.

"What are those?" I asked a sailor.

"Barf bags," he replied.

As the catamaran swayed back and forth on the choppy waters, I felt nauseous for the first (and only) boating time. And now cruise ships have made sightseeing tours to Tulum barf-free: They transport passengers in tenders (small boats), not swaying catamarans.

In addition to visiting the spectacular multi-stepped Mayan structures, the journey to Tulum was memorable for a negative reason. It featured a lot of waiting in line, during which Larry and I were forced to listen to a young teen girl complain to her parents about everything. Later in the cruise, the ship held a passenger talent show and Miss Whiny transformed into Miss American Idol, singing a beautiful rendition of "The Rose." Who could have known?

———

Larry and I took our first cruise in the early 1970s when sea vacations were popular just with senior citizens. As a result, on the *Rotterdam* we became friends with the only two other young couples.

It was a two-week Caribbean cruise and we booked the cheapest accommodations: a tiny inside cabin with bunk beds. The room was claustrophobic and the lack of windows made it dark and depressing. As a result, Larry and I decided to splurge on outside rooms for future cruises.

Cabins with small round portholes, which provided light but didn't open, were fine for our next few voyages. Then, several years later, we were upgraded to a room with a balcony. And this wasn't an ordinary balcony. Our cabin was at the extreme rear of the ship (the stern), in the middle of a row of suites. The long attached balcony with two full-length lounge chairs gave us a clear backwards view of undulating waves as our ship glided through the ocean.

Since that awesome experience, we've only booked cabins with balconies. Unfortunately, however, none of our subsequent balconies have been as large or as private as the glorious first one.

———

Because I love to swim, I always use the ship's pool. While most passengers just hang out in the water—cooling off, sipping drinks, and chatting with others—I actually swim, doing laps.

Sometimes that's easy. One of our boats had a small indoor lap pool. Although I prefer swimming outside, I was able to do my laps on that ship without inconveniencing anyone.

Other times, however, swimming laps is more challenging. One of our cruise ships had a round pool. But even then, I managed to swim circular laps.

———

In the late 1980s, Larry and I took a cruise from California to the Mexican Riviera, which my husband calls, "the cruise I don't remember."

Larry felt dizzy the day before our departure so he had a CT scan to make sure he was well enough to travel. When the scan didn't reveal a problem, the doctor theorized Larry had suffered a touch of heat stroke after exercising in the hot gym. "You should feel better in a day or two," he said, clearing Larry for the cruise. So off we went.

Unfortunately, the doctor was wrong; Larry didn't feel better.

On that cruise, we were assigned seats at a large round table with a tour operator and his family and friends.

The good part: We didn't have to make conversation because our tablemates all knew each other. The bad part: Each night, the tour guy ordered wine for everyone at our table. But I don't like wine and Larry, who loves wine, couldn't have alcohol because of his brain fog.

Another unfortunate happening was that although our cabin was adjacent to the gym, Larry was in no condition to exercise. He walked so slowly that when we took the ship's staircases, I had to stop at each landing and wait for him to catch up.

When we reached the Mexican ports, our touring choices were limited. Larry and I sat around a hotel's pool in Puerto

Vallarta and again on the beach at Mazatlan. I was able to swim, but I didn't do much else. Larry didn't feel well until the vacation was over and we were back home.

———

Larry and I have each had memorable experiences on our cruises. On the Mexican island of Cozumel, I did my Lucy Ricardo imitation, stepping into a sidewalk of wet concrete. Why? There was no sign saying "Do Not Enter," so I entered.

Another time, as we were exiting the ship in New York to go home, customs officials in front of the gangplank called to passengers: "Any fruits or vegetables?"

"No, thanks," Larry said, smiling at the men. "I couldn't eat another thing."

We were immediately removed from the line and forced to remain on the ship for another half hour while humorless customs workers rummaged through our luggage looking for contraband.

The following year, a customs employee tried to joke with Larry. But my husband didn't kid back; he'd learned his lesson.

———

On our most recent cruise, Larry and I got a premonition of the future. Because the air inside ships is stagnant, these big boats are great breeding grounds for germs and many voyages suffer norovirus outbreaks.

On our cruise, about fifty passengers (out of 3,000) caught a stomach bug and were quarantined inside their cabins. Although the rest of us weren't hampered, we were slightly inconvenienced: All public bathroom doors remained open so we wouldn't touch handles and dining room tables were bare, with no tablecloths or condiments. During meals, we received sealed packets of salt and pepper and had to ask waiters for ketchup or mustard.

When we docked at ports, our ship posted a big "QUARANTINED" sign next to the gangplank and only passengers and crew—no guests—were allowed on board.

We laughed about our experience then, taking photos of ourselves in front of the sign. But this was before the tragic COVID-19 pandemic and that cruising experience seems much less funny now.

CAKE FIX

I needed a custom cake for my daughter's bridal shower and I wanted Bernadine to make it. Bernadine, a talented artist who worked with me at the *PennySaver*, was also a gifted baker.

Since Merri was a sales rep for the Yellow Pages (remember when people used phone directory books?), Larry and I thought her cake should resemble an ad for that publication. After I explained the details to Bernadine, she agreed to bake the cake and then deliver it to me in the parking lot of Yorktown's Burger King the morning of the shower.

But when Bernadine arrived at the lot and opened the box to show me the cake, she grimaced and cried, "Oh, no!"

"What's wrong?" I asked. The cake looked terrific, just like a real Yellow Pages ad with the shower invitation covering most of the "page" and phony filler text, which Bernadine called "Greeken," comprising the rest.

"It must have happened when I hit the speed bump on Allen Avenue," Bernadine said, pointing to some of the delicate basket-weave stitches along the side that were now somewhat mushy.

"It's okay," I said, remembering I had to be at the shower venue before noon. "The top of the cake is fine. Nobody will notice anything."

"No, it's not fine," Bernadine argued. "I can't give you a damaged cake. I have to fix it."

"But we don't have enough time," I said. Bernadine lived in Peekskill, a half hour away, so for her to travel back and forth to repair the cake would have taken well over an hour.

"Can we fix it at my house?" I asked.

"You don't have the tools I need," she said. "But I know what to do. We'll go to Joyce's house."

Joyce, another *PennySaver* artist who was also a terrific cake designer and baker, lived near me in Yorktown. Luckily, the two baker-artists were good friends.

So that's what we did. We went to Joyce's house and in fifteen minutes Bernadine and Joyce repaired the delicate basket-weave stitches on the side of my daughter's cake.

The cake arrived at the bridal shower in perfect condition, was admired by everyone, and then eaten. In addition to looking beautiful, the cake was delicious.

TRIAL AND ERRORS

If a pedestrian is hit by a bus, should the court award him lots of money?

That's the question I had to answer as a juror in a civil trial in White Plains in February of 2012.

The Liberty Lines bus, traveling with no passengers at a low speed, was headed to its nearby Yonkers garage in April of 2008 when it hit Mr. B, the 40-year-old plaintiff from nearby Mount Vernon. Although Mr. B was in the marked intersection, he may have stepped out when the bus hit him. Mr. B said he had the green light, but both the bus driver and a witness in a car opposite the bus said their signal was green.

Mr. B claimed he was thrown from the bus and was in and out of consciousness, injuring his left side. However, EMS records stated he was fully conscious with no visible injuries.

He was taken to Jacobi Hospital, tested, kept overnight, and then released. Mr. B, who ironically was also a bus driver—for a school— claimed he could no longer drive a bus full-time or for long periods because of pain and weakness on his left side and two permanently numbed fingers.

Mr. B's lawyer, Mr. R, was a 78-year-old (he told us his age) overweight man with a thick Bronx accent. Picture an incompetent, older combination of Joe Pesci in *My Cousin Vinny* and Peter Falk in "Columbo." All the jurors felt he hadn't been inside a courtroom in many years.

Mr. R apologized for being unable to stand to examine witnesses because of a bad back. But he also couldn't hear well. At one point, Mr. R asked the judge what had just been said.

"Nothing," the judge explained. "I coughed."

"Oh," Mr. R said. "I thought you were yellin' at me again. You're always yellin' at me."

Although the judge never yelled at the plaintiff's attorney, the bus company's lawyer constantly objected to Mr. R's questions and nearly all the objections were sustained.

The case took three days: Wednesday, Thursday, and Friday. Justice moved slowly then, thanks partly to ninety-minute lunch breaks instituted by New York State to save money on salaries.

On the first day, we heard testimony from three people: Mr. B; the accused bus driver; and a witness, who was a mechanic for the bus company.

It's an understatement to say Mr. B wasn't a credible witness because he lied about nearly everything: his criminal record (he had been arrested for being in a stolen car in Virginia), the accident, his consciousness, the distance he landed from the bus, his injuries, and even his job applications.

He claimed he needed medication to get through the day and had to be helped to travel to and from the court. However, several jurors saw him walking with no problem and moving his arms freely. He apparently carried a cane (which I never saw), but another juror saw him playing with it.

After listening to Wednesday's testimony, we deliberated late that afternoon to assign blame and found 65/35 for Mr. B since, despite his lies, the bus did hit him.

The second part of the case involved assigning damages. On Thursday, Mr. B again testified about his injuries and we also heard from Dr. S, a physiologist who had been treating him. Mr. B owed her $10,000 and she had a lien on the court case for payment.

Dr. S tried to prove Mr. B's neck ailment was a result of the accident, although he didn't complain about the pain until March of 2010. Then we learned that in March of 2009, Mr. B had been a passenger in a car involved in an accident—and at that time filed a complaint about neck pain.

On Friday morning, two doctors testified for the defense. A neurologist (paid $4,000 for his testimony) had examined Mr. B the previous year and found no neurological damage—including no numbed fingers. Next, an orthopedic surgeon (paid $7,000 for his testimony) confirmed the first doctor's findings of no neurological damage.

Although the case ended just before 4 pm Friday afternoon, we were ordered to make our decisions by 4:20 so we could leave at 4:30. (After we had stayed in court until 4:45 on Wednesday to decide the first part of the case, the chief judge had reprimanded our judge for lateness—and we couldn't adjourn until Monday because two of the six jurors were unable to return.)

So we worked quickly. Because of Mr. B's lies, we didn't award him much money.

For being hit by the bus (pain and suffering), four jury members (including me), wanted to give Mr. B $5,000, but one juror didn't want to award him any money and another wanted to give him just $3,000. We settled on $3,500.

We also gave Mr. B about three months of his annual salary ($7,500) for time missed right after the accident and awarded him $2,200 for unpaid medical bills.

We didn't award Mr. B any money for future problems because we felt his serious injuries (if he had any) didn't stem from the bus accident. He hired his lawyer after his car accident the following year.

Our conclusion: Mr. B was looking for an easy way to make money out of an old bus accident he had been lucky to walk away from.

WORKING (MOSTLY 9 - 5)

MY ONE-YEAR TEACHING CAREER

When I was a little girl and people asked me what I wanted to be when I grew up, I always gave the same response: "a teacher."

More specifically, I hoped to teach kids in fourth or fifth grade. To meet this goal, I majored in elementary education at Queens College and after graduation, got a job in P.S. 138 in the Bronx, near the Castle Hill projects, my childhood home.

The school building was fairly new and the neighborhood was still integrated and lower-middle class. It seemed like a good place to start a teaching career.

But it wasn't. The year was 1968, the height of the Vietnam War, a time men could avoid being drafted into the army by becoming teachers. I didn't complain being assigned a class of second-graders because an older man, another new teacher, was also given a second-grade class.

In addition, September—the start of the school year—marked the beginning of New York City's infamous 36-day teachers' strike. During that time, teachers weren't paid so Larry and I needed alternative jobs. I knew how to type so I worked as an office temp. Since Larry had no office skills, he became a Burns Guard, protecting the Silvercup bread factory overlooking Shea Stadium in Flushing (in case anyone wanted dough).

When teachers finally returned to the classrooms in early November, we had to work an extra 45 minutes each day to make up for all the lost time. That was tough enough for an experienced teacher, but it was terrible for me. I had the bottom second-grade class: None of my thirty students knew how to read.

Many of the kids in my class had serious problems that impacted their learning. I remember three students well: John, a tall and lanky 7-year-old, epitomized perpetual motion. Today he'd probably be diagnosed as having severe ADHD because he acted out constantly, disrupting the class.

José didn't speak one word all year. He thought he was an airplane, making buzzing noises as he spread his wings to propel himself around the classroom.

And poor Julie was even more damaged. She sat at her desk quietly sticking pencils into various parts of her body.

I tried to get help for those children and others, but was unsuccessful. The following year, however, ten students from my class were placed in junior guidance, the 1960s version of special education.

But by then it was too late for me. I was finished with teaching, both mentally and physically, having been sick much of that school year, probably due to stress. I turned in my teaching certificate and became a newspaper reporter, a job I loved.

DIARY OF A YOUNG REPORTER

Many years ago, as a retail reporter/editor for *Daily News Record (DNR)*, a now-defunct men's wear and textile trade newspaper, I kept a journal. Here are the highlights:

Preface: December 21, 1970

Working at Fairchild Publications [then located at 12th Street & Fifth Avenue in New York City, on the edge of Greenwich Village] is a unique experience. After only a short time, I became aware that the people, events, and company policies were fascinating, so I decided to keep a one-year diary. Since I arrived at this decision in mid-December, I was going to wait till January to start—but the pre-Christmas days were too good to lose.

Tuesday, December 22

Major event of the day: the paean's party (as Howard dubbed it) came off with an unusual incident: Herb asked Howard if he might have a drink with us. What could Howard say?

But Herb didn't come to the party. Instead, he ate a sandwich in the office. (First time any of us saw that.) Was it to make us feel guilty for not including him? Did he expect us to include him because of his marriage today? We'll never know.

However, Herb did have a drink downstairs with Kevin and stopped upstairs to say he couldn't stay for a drink with us.

[Herb Blueweiss, *DNR*'s publisher, was a short, jovial man in his mid 40s who never seemed to do anything but read the newspaper and make phone calls.]

[Howard Kissel, sportswear reporter/editor, was a tall and lanky man in his late 20s with curly, long brown hair. He loved the theater, hated writing about men's sweaters, and eventually secured his dream job: drama critic for the *New York Daily News*.]

[Kevin, a textile reporter in his late 20s, was our resident villain: the company snitch. He even had both a goatee and a devilish grin.]

We took 2 1/2 hours for lunch and Herman [textile editor]—who calls me "Miss (sic) Berliner"—was the only executive present. I guess he figures he can be reckless since he's retiring next month.

On the way back in the elevator, we luncheoners met Jerry and burst into song: "We wish you a Jerry Kriska, we wish you a Jerry Kriska, we wish you a Jerry Kriska, and a Herbie Blueweiss!"

[Jerry Kriska, features editor, was a crotchety, pipe-smoking man in his 60s who never praised anyone's work and intimidated most of the young reporters, including me.]

Wednesday, December 23

Herb was back in the office at 11 today. Theories:

1. Mary Lou's job is important (unlike Herb's), so she has no time for a honeymoon.

2. Herb doesn't trust us with his presents and he's afraid we'll steal them. If so, I think he's right. The way we ogle each other's gifts (not mine. I don't have any), maybe we would take

the loot.

Herb's wedding (I should say Mary Lou's) made the *New York Times*. Her father is a retired carpet exec. The write-up was strange in that Herb's first marriage and daughter weren't mentioned. It sounded like he was a 25-year-old newlywed.

I got my second Christmas card today, doubling last year's output by 200 percent. This card came with envelope opened, card folded backwards, from an agency I never heard of, and was signed illegibly. But I was pleased—which shows my standards.

Thursday, December 24

Kiddy Day with John's and Matt's [textile reporter] sons visiting. The latter tried a number trick on me and, of course, I couldn't get the answer. Then he tried it on John, who figured it out. The boy told everyone that "Susan's husband" was the only one who figured out the trick. Bill T corrected the boy, telling him John was my father.

[John, associate editor in charge of apparel and retailing, was my immediate boss. He was a balding, heavyset Italian in his late 40s who knew everything that went on in *DNR*. Loud and opinionated, he was liked by many and disliked by some. I liked him very much.]

[Bill T, news editor, was a charismatic guy in his mid 30s who strutted around the office. Knowledgeable about all things *DNR*, he was a good friend of John's.]

Wednesday, December 30

Dick had a bunch of robes out for his pajama issue. Two were black and white velours, so before lunch Bill T and Al tried them on. They looked like a couple of boxers. Not to be outdone, John put on a cartoon robe, and looked like a fat Japanese wrestler. It would have made a beautiful picture—

and a lifetime blackmail racket.

[Dick, furnishings (shirts & ties) reporter/editor, was a short and pudgy status-seeker in his late 20s. His openness about his desire to climb up the social ladder endeared him to the rest of us.]

[Al, special sections editor, was a handsome man in his late 40s and another close friend of John's.]

Wednesday, January 6

Dick announced he was leaving us and joining *Town & Country*, a step up society-wise. His timing was excellent because Sandy and John had just had a meeting and decided how to reorganize the apparel department when Dick dropped his bombshell. Back to the drawing board.

[Sandy, managing editor, was a quiet, decent-looking balding guy in his early 30s. But Sandy had zero personality and it was difficult to hold a conversation with him.]

I finally finished my West Side 6-7 [two-page feature story]. Jerry kidded me about it, saying he didn't like it and would make it a BTL [Between the Lines - short blurbs]. The story is 12 and 1/2 takes [pages].

Thursday, January 7

In the morning, I went to a Bureau of Advertising screening and an obnoxious reporter squeezed next to me, saying, "I have to sit next to Audrey." When he introduced himself, I recognized his name from the *New York Times*' Sunday advertising column. The few *Times* people I've met are loud, obnoxious, and extremely impressed with themselves.

Lunch with Kevin, Mary Lois, and Howard. Items discussed: (1) Kevin's outburst with Herb J yesterday because Herb J was upset with Kevin's 3-sentence stories. To get even, Kevin wrote a very long, complex ("but grammatically correct") sentence. (He's an ex-English teacher.)

Herb J realized the "joke" (Kevin's jokes are never funny) and said to him, "What do you think I am, a horse's ass?"

"I don't know," Kevin replied. "What does a horse's ass look like?"

[Mary Lois, in her late 20s, covered fashion fabrics—the only woman in the textile department. She was from Alabama, with a Southern drawl, and this was her second stint with *DNR*. Remarried with a daughter from her previous marriage, Mary Lois loved the theater and routinely got chastised for gravitating to Howard's desk.]

[Herb J, a textiles editor, was a gangly, balding man in his 30s who reminded me of a country bumpkin.]

(2) The apparel realignment. I suggested Gerry, in textiles, might be moved in since no one new was being hired. Howard pointed out that our publisher [a former furnishings editor] would be the logical one to take over. "He knows the market and has nothing to do."

[Gerry was a quiet, unassuming guy in his mid-20s with a deadpan sense of humor. When he grew a beard and no one acknowledged it, Gerry explained: "I have the kind of face that people don't look at."]

(3) Howard calculated the drop in *DNR* staff in his four years here: When he came, there were 33 employees and now there are 22.

Friday, January 8

I guessed right. Gerry was named furnishings editor today. Fairchild actually made the right decision.

Gerry's got one of the best motivations to lose weight: to fit into sample sizes. How Gerry's machinery section is going to be split up, nobody knows. One thing's for sure: Nobody's being hired.

Interviewing customers at the Conspiracy boutique in the afternoon, I met a celebrity: a member of the rock group, The Five Stairsteps of "O-o-h Child" fame.

Jerry apparently liked my "West Side Store-y" 6-7. Both Peggy and Rich told me they overheard Jerry tell Sandy what a good job I did.

[Peggy and Rich were hired on the same day as me in September, 1969. For Peggy, career apparel and accessories reporter/editor, this was her first job. Since we were both short brunettes and close in age, some Fairchild employees confused the two of us.]

[Rich, fashion editor, was a good-looking bachelor in his early 30s who was well versed with Manhattan's nightlife.]

Monday, January 11

A great example of Fairchild organization: Kathie reminded me in the morning that we'd never gotten word on what we were supposed to do at the NRMA [National Retail Merchants Association] show tomorrow. Sandy and John were in Philadelphia for a retirement luncheon for a long-time reporter, so we called our Philadelphia bureau.

It was a good thing we did. John told us to be at the Hilton at 8:45. Kathie and I would have come into the office at 10 if we hadn't called.

[Kathie, boys' wear reporter/editor, was an attractive and quiet blonde with an engaging laugh. She was in her mid-20s.]

Tuesday, January 12

What a day! As Howard would say, today I gave my 100 percent and Kathie did too. We both interviewed retailers twice at the NRMA—once after a seminar, once before the BAMA [Boys and Men's Apparel Association] luncheon. And they were all store presidents. When I got back to the office (after 1 pm), Bill T decided he wanted to use the interview for Wednesday so I had to write the lead.

Kathie came back after the luncheon and wrote the speech story. Then Herb decided he wanted to do the store president 6-7 for Thursday. That meant Kathie and I had to (1) identify the pictures (2) write our quotes so Fred [art director] would know the amount of copy (3) wait for the pictures to be enlarged.

Kathie and I both left the office at 6 pm after a nine-hour day (with 15 minutes for lunch). And tomorrow we still have to write the lead for the 6-7.

My Monday NRMA story was used in *Women's Wear Daily* (*WWD*) because our paper was too tight.

Wednesday, January 13:

Another 100 percent day. In the morning, Kathie and I found that Fred had misspelled two names in the layout. The changes had to be sent down as separate cuts [captions] and we had to explain the situation to Marty in Willingboro [southern New Jersey plant where *DNR* was printed].

Kathie wrote the lead for the story, John revised it, and Sandy approved it. We had to make duplicate dummies because Willingboro lost Tuesday's 6-7.

Related developments: Herb sent Kathie and me a note, congratulating us for talking to all those big shots. (I wondered why he kept smiling at me during the pre-lunch reception.) Then he added something like, "I'm looking forward to seeing the great story in tomorrow's *DNR*."

Kathie and I both felt the same thing: instant added pressure, since we hadn't finished writing the story. Herb probably did mean it as a compliment, but I'd rather be thanked after, not before or during.

In the afternoon, the president of Macy's Corp. resigned and I had to write a backup story in case the *WWD* writer didn't finish his in time for our deadline. He didn't, so my story ran.

Thursday, January 14

My 6-7 (actually an 8-9) ran today and the layout, quotes, and name spelling turned out fine. In fact, everything looked great except the introduction. Instead of being in 12-point type, it was in about 5-point. I hope our readers have magnifying glasses.

At the real last minute, Howard took up a collection for Dick, who's leaving tomorrow. Dick didn't want a luncheon and we couldn't give him one in the style he would like to be accustomed to.

Next week I have to interview groups of retailers twice—at the Boutique Show and MRA [Menswear Retailers of America]. It shapes up as one big headache.

Friday, January 15

For Dick's going-away present, somebody found a two-inch wide purple tie. We presented it to him (along with a $50 gift certificate to Mark Cross) and he wore the tie for the rest of the afternoon.

Peggy was back after three days in the Bahamas for the Career Apparel Show. She asked me if anyone had said anything about her stories. I said "no," but they must have been good since they all ran on page 1. She said Sandy told her she did a good job, but Herb hadn't even welcomed her back.

At Fairchild, if no one says anything, you can assume you're doing a good job.

Monday, January 18

First thing in the morning, I went to the New Yorker to interview buyers attending the MAC [Men's Apparel Club] show. There was only one problem: There was no show, only a dinner tonight. Another Fairchild boner, though not in a class with the yacht race fiasco, when I spent a day at a Connecticut dock with a photographer waiting for an America's Cup yacht that never returned.

Herb asked John to help him write a guest column for Clara. Why does Clara need a guest column written? Nobody knows. One thing's for sure, she's not sick. Clara's never sick. If someone calls, Dee has strict orders to say Clara is "out in the market."

One other thing's for sure: When Clara's in the office, you can't miss her because her feet clatter. As John says, we need a runway for Clara.

[Clara Hancox, *DNR* columnist and long-time employee, was a petite 50ish brunette who was also very loud—think mini-Ethel Merman—both in person and on the phone. For more about Clara, see "Lady Legend," p. 145]

[Dee, Sandy's and Bill T's secretary, was in her mid 20s, competent and attractive, with flowing blonde hair. However, she was grossly obese. Several years later, when I returned to *DNR* for a visit, she had lost lots of weight and looked terrific.]

Tuesday, January 19

Word is Kathie and I are going to Philly on Sunday night through Tuesday, with Gerry and Howard going Friday night through Sunday. The general feeling is that Sandy and John want to take it easy at the MRA after working hard last year. It should be pure chaos.

It was 4 degrees today and we couldn't get enough steam. Cool air was coming out of the air conditioning vents and I worked part of the day with gloves on.

WWD was all lit up by ABC-TV cameras. It's becoming the norm. I heard the interviewer ask with a straight face: "Mr.

Brady, what do you think about the hot pants?"

[James Brady, a New York celebrity, was publisher of *Women's Wear Daily*. When I was first hired, he was also group vice-president of *DNR* and would shake my hand at the entrance to our holiday parties, although he never knew my name.]

Wednesday, January 20

Gerry is making great progress as furnishings editor. Today, he got five free shirts after wearing a button-down so manufacturers would take pity on him. But Gerry said Herb got 12 shirts each from two manufacturers.

I tried to get the staff to help me think of a head for the 6-7 I seem to be handling by myself with Sandy away (in Dallas, hiring a new reporter) and John doing Bill T's work. We came up with "The Son Also Retails," "The Rising Son," "Inherit the Store," "Next in Line," and "Retailing: Second Generation." Sandy loves colon titles, so I bet he'll use that one. [He didn't. The story was titled "all in the family."]

Thursday, January 21

I found out Herb was upset that we were making noise yesterday (about the 6-7 heads) and wanted John to quiet us. It was 5:15 and even if we were enjoying ourselves, it was *DNR* business.

John stuck up for us, telling Herb he shouldn't complain about our noise when "another party" (Kevin) was causing an uproar. Kevin had screamed about his story not going on page 1.

Barbara Walters of NBC was the "hot pants" interviewer today. I can't wait to see what *WWD* thinks of next.

John's guest column for Clara ran today. In small print, it was explained that, "Clara Hancox is away." How's that for clarity?

The new president of Fairchild's name is Sias—or as we are saying, Tsuris [trouble], which is probably what he'll have.

Friday, January 22

Howard wore a sweater today and Herb asked him where his tie was. It's interesting that Kevin is never asked that question.

John asked me if I wanted to work Sunday and cover the Boutique Show. I didn't.

Nice lunch with the young retailers I interviewed at N.Y.U. I sat with guys from Boston, Virginia, Texas, Seattle, and Rhode Island.

Afterwards, I found out Bob from *Men's Wear* [Fairchild's monthly magazine] was there and walked back to the office with him. We started talking about the Boutique Show, which led to the Amy [*Men's Wear* reporter] house ad in the magazine.

I mentioned that we at *DNR* loved the ad and recited our favorite line: Amy "lives, breathes, and swings in the world of boutiques."

"We originally had 'sleeps' in there," Bob said, "but Mort [editor] made us take it out."

Tuesday, January 26

There are times *DNR* can actually look good—like when it's compared to imitation publications. At the Boutique Show, I picked up several papers that tried to imitate *DNR* and *WWD*.

Jerry went to the Boutique Show with no one knowing about it. (As John says, there are two papers: *DNR* and Jerry. He's an independent operation.) Now Rich has to send a photographer. It's a good thing Sandy and John didn't want me to do a photo layout on boutique retailers because Jerry's pictures ran in BTLs today.

Jerry picked on me late in the afternoon.

Jerry: "Susan, you and I are going to have a fight."

Howard: "Good. Can we get tickets?"

Jerry was mad because I didn't retype our St. Louis reporter's page 1 story. I explained it was six-pages and I did it late in the day. Jerry was annoyed she penciled in corrections.

Wednesday, January 27

Herb came into the office carrying about 10 boxes of shirts. (I don't exaggerate.) He told us he was giving the new shirts to his brother. Then he gave some of them to Gerry. (They wear the same size.) Gerry thought the shirts had been worn and laundered. We always wondered what Herb did after he wore a shirt once.

Thursday, January 28

This really happened: At 5:30, John, Sandy, Bill T, and I were getting on our coats and Herb was in his seat when John Fairchild sauntered in. "Herb," he said. "What are you doing about hot pants?"

(We all stood still, listening.) Herb said we were calling them "short shorts" and had mentioned them in our Boutique Show stories.

"Why don't you call them hot pants?" Fairchild asked. "After all, it's a Fairchild term and everybody—even the *New York Times*—uses it. I called Charlotte Curtis at the *Times* today and said, 'Hello, Charlotte Curtis Hot Pants.' She said she had bought some."

Then Fairchild took out a drawing of men's hot pants. (I think they were lederhosen and Egyptian shorts.) "It's not new," he said. "The Austrians had them, only these are shorter. I think they're going to be very big for spring and you should do some double-page spreads for them."

He added that he thought the term "hot pants" was necessary for us to use. "After all, that's what they are. They're certainly not cool pants and they're very masculine."

During that time, I was finding it difficult to keep from laughing. First, especially with the drawing, I thought he was kidding. But he was dead serious.

Walking to the subway with Sandy and Bill, Sandy was already thinking of how to get hot pants into a 6-7. I guess it had to happen. But this way?

[John Fairchild, whose family owned our newspapers before selling them to Capital Cities, was company chairman and at that time had an office adjacent to *DNR*. He was tall, in his late 40s, well dressed, with prematurely white hair.]

Friday, January 29

We saw an *HFD* [*Home Furnishings Daily*] staff report: editor and publisher letters sent to the workers. That's the one thing we lack—a hard-hitting publisher or editor memo to us. But *HFD* must be better than I thought because John says they think it's hysterical.

The three dailies can best be described this way: *WWD* staffers act serious and take themselves seriously; *HFD* staffers act serious and don't take themselves seriously; and *DNR* staffers don't act serious and don't take themselves seriously. But by most people's standards, we're the best paper, quality-wise.

Monday, February 1

It was really freezing today. I even tried typing with gloves. (It didn't work.) All the men had their jackets on, very formal looking. When I told Sig [textile reporter] that he looked good, he took me seriously. At least he didn't argue. No one wants to talk to Sig because he debates everything.

My favorite Sig story: I saw him reading the *New York Times* one day and asked, "Anything interesting?"

His response: "Anything interesting? In the *New York Times*!"

I had to call stores about Rockefeller's new budget and when I got an answer from Alexander's PR [public relations] agency, I did my story and then, as a favor, gave it to *WWD*. After looking at the story, the *WWD* guy asked who gave me the information. When he heard it was the agency, he threw it back at me, saying, "We don't want that!"

He was really rude. I wish I'd had the courage to reply with something nasty. After all, I was doing him a favor. Later, when I reached a Lord & Taylor vice-chairman, I didn't give him my story. Just a little revenge.

Tuesday, February 2

Sandy invited me to lunch today. I probably was his last choice. He had a lunch date with a manufacturer of big men's clothing and Bill B, the logical choice, couldn't go. In ten-degree weather, we had to walk ten blocks to Pete's Tavern. But I was able to have a discussion with Sandy, an improvement over last year's subway ride when I couldn't think of anything to say.

[Bill B, suits reporter/editor, originally from Boston, was in his late 40s and had the distinction of being the oldest apparel reporter. Short and dapper, he hung out with John and Bill T, but, unlike them, wasn't part of management.]

Thursday, February 4

We finally had our pre-MRA meeting and they sort of told us what we are doing. But I have nothing to do Monday morning. ("Go around and talk to retailers," Sandy said. "About what?" I asked.) Everyone else has specific questions to ask manufacturers.

Sunday, February 7

Philadelphia greeted Kathie and me with hail on Sunday night. We checked into the Holiday Inn and found Gerry and Howard's note to us, suggesting two restaurants, so we went to the original Bookbinder's.

The best moment was when this girl walked in escorted by four guys. Her dress had the lowest neckline I've ever seen in public. The whole restaurant turned in one motion to look. It was like a comedy routine—waiters almost fell over tables.

Monday, February 8

After Kathie and I went to Sandy and John's room for a briefing, we all grabbed a cab to the Civic Center. Once inside, we went to our booth and I got a chance to see Ginny again. Like me, she had nothing to do in the morning so the two of us walked around the convention hall with John.

[Tall, thin, and in her mid-20s, Ginny (Virginia) was our Philadelphia reporter and my closest *DNR* friend. We spoke often on the phone and even corresponded by mail for several years after I left the newspaper in 1973.]

Ginny and I were both supposed to go to a Botany luncheon. But John wanted someone to interview college students who were MRA guests so she and I did that together. We were going to eat with the students, but after drinking soup from plastic bowls and taking a few bites out of a horrible beef-gravy-roll concoction, we looked at each other and said, "Why are we doing this? We don't have to eat here." We grabbed a taxi to the Botany luncheon.

Back at the Civic Center, Kathie and Rich had tried typing their stories in the booth, but the typewriter was broken and they had no copy paper. Good planning. Both their stories were saved for the next day.

At the hotel, Kathie and I got ready for the formal Lulu

awards dinner. John, Kathie, Bill B, and I sat together and then a *New York Times* guy and a few PR people joined us. The *Times* guy was overly loud and obnoxious. Every time he laughed, he banged into the table and eventually spilled a drink.

The Lulu fashion awards were doled out by Eddy Arnold [country music singer] and done much like the Oscars. The awards were for consumer papers, but *Pontiac Press*, also owned by Capital Cities, was one of the winners.

Tuesday, February 9

I got the typewriter from Sandy and Kathie, went to the Civic Center, and wrote my story. Sandy came by about noon and approved the lead, but I forgot to ask him what to do with the typewriter so I left it in the Philadelphia office.

At the Civic Center later, I covered the boutique seminar with Amy of *Men's Wear*. Ginny stopped in and complimented Amy on one of her articles. "How'd you learn about his sex life?" Ginny asked her.

"We always test our information first," Amy said.

Kathie and I caught the 6:13 train (with many other MRAers) and I got home about 9.

Wednesday, February 10

A day of comparing MRA gossip as well as writing stories. Rich was supposed to call Howard and Gerry for dinner Saturday night, but fell asleep. Bill B left the room, but didn't close the door. Rich woke up at 2 am to find John and Sandy staring at him. He doesn't know how many people had been in and out of the room while he was sleeping.

Herb and Mary Lou (she left before we arrived) had a fight in the hall one evening. Herb yelled, "Maybe I remarried too soon!"

All morning, we waited for the return of Sandy, John, Bill B, and Rich. They walked in just when a bunch of us came back from lunch.

Bill looked and felt great and said it started the night before. "I felt awful until Rich gave me an aspirin," he explained. "I've been my old self ever since."

Rich wouldn't admit the "aspirin" was really a pep pill, but smiled mysteriously.

I saw the new *Men's Wear* in the afternoon and there was a great article called "The Women Behind the Men," about the wives of *Men's Wear* staffers. All the women seemed the same — young, hard-faced, shallow, obnoxious. *DNR* looks better all the time.

Men's Wear's cover story was on Barney's ads, an interview with Jack Byrne. Now my story can wait. They also interviewed Paul Stuart's display man, who I talked to last week. I wish he'd told me *Men's Wear* had been there.

Thursday, February 11

I heard a great MRA story. Mike, our Philadelphia ad man, got into a fight with a New York *DNR* ad man at an MRA function. One of them spit at the other and they started fighting with folding chairs.

The New York ad man was fired, but Mike wasn't. He seems to be a great guy: carries a club in his car because he has a bad temper.

Gerry, riding in Mike's car during the convention, asked: "Why do you carry a club?"

"To hit pricks," Mike said, adding he keeps an oar in his other car.

Friday, February 12

I questioned John about the ad guys' fight. Like usual, John knew all the information, even though he didn't witness it. The fight occurred at Sunday night's Trevira dinner when the very drunk New York guy made obscene comments to a girl at the table. Also, one of them accused the other of stealing advertising.

We spent part of the afternoon doing the *New York Magazine* contest: "If _____ married _____, she'd be _____. Peggy came up with a good one: "If Anouk Aimee married King Farouk, she'd be Anouk Farouk." Mine (which I'm going to enter): "If Pet Clark marries George Raft, Sigmund Freud, and Steve Forrest, she'd be Pet Raft Freud Forrest." [It got Honorable Mention.]

Wednesday, February 17

We have nobody doing retail stuff in Washington DC anymore and that leaves a Retail Market category open. I said it wouldn't be fair to stick Ginny with another area to cover, so I'm afraid I'll get stuck doing it. Sometimes it doesn't pay to be nice.

Thursday, February 18

More economy moves. The amount of stringers [freelancers] we can use is down to about ten. Thank God, Kathleen [Birmingham, Alabama prolific retail correspondent with professional glossy photos] is one of them. Also, they are only taking one car trip a day to Willingboro now (too expensive for gas, tolls, etc.), which makes getting pictures out a real hassle for us.

Friday, February 19

I stayed in the office late because Larry and I were seeing *1776* on Broadway. I told Herb (after he asked me why I didn't go home) and he said he'd seen the play.

"How did you like it?" I asked.

"I don't remember," he said. "I saw it so long ago, it was with my first wife."

Herb liked that comment so much, he repeated it to John.

Monday, February 22

Today's *DNR* was a mess. The second graph of my story (page 2) was all muddled. I got the original copy and found that Joe [copy desk chief] had "edited" my story and added the words that made it wrong.

What happened with Gerry's (lead) story was worse: 5% was changed to 51%—again the copy desk's goof.

[The copy desk was actually a circle of desks, like satellites around a planet. Joe, who used two braces to walk due to polio, sat in the interior (planet) seat and assigned stories to the proofreaders, who also wrote headlines for all articles except page 1 and 6-7 features.]

Wednesday, February 24

The tension in *DNR* was almost unbearable. It seems yesterday's Apparel-Retail "meeting" was nothing more than a class lecture on discipline. I'm glad I missed it (dentist appointment). The apparel department was told to cut down on lengthy office talks among one another and to stop singing and laughing.

Howard took it as a personal attack and he's probably right. I'm sure the lecture was meant for him.

Another of the company's brilliant moves: *DNR*'s artists moved into our area. The whole art department is being split up this way, which is basically a good idea, but we're supposed to be moving to the fourth floor in a couple of weeks. Why couldn't they wait till then?

Our art staff set themselves up interestingly: Straights in one area and fags in another area. They hate this setup and do have one legitimate gripe—poor lighting.

Thursday, February 25

It was my turn to have a tension-filled day—a Spartans Industries stockholders' meeting that lasted from 10 to 2. Carole from *HFD*, a *New York Times* guy, and John from our Financial Department were there too. So was this woman, Evelyn Davis, one of a breed of professional stockholders' meeting attendees. [Her *New York Times* obituary called her a "Shareholder Scourge of C.E.O.s."]

Davis wore "$11.75" hot pants purchased "at Korvette's" [discount store owned by Spartans]. She introduced herself to all the press and asked if we had a photographer. (She also called *WWD* yesterday.)

Davis hogged the microphone, kept interrupting, and finally got into a name-calling contest with another woman.

The Gilbert brothers (also professionals at this) and a few other idiots helped prolong the meeting. Many stockholders did have legitimate points, but things were repeated over and over because the speakers loved to listen to themselves talk.

Afterwards, when all four of us press people converged on the board chairman, he refused to talk to anyone from Fairchild. "You're a scandal sheet!" he shouted. "You only print lies!"

When I returned to the office, ate a 5-minute lunch and told Bill T what happened, he told me to look at my typewriter. Inside was his note that Herb wanted me to call Bonwit's about a new boutique for a BTL. According to Bill T, that was first in importance.

I also had to do my dummy and John's, plus be introduced to out-of-town Fairchild News Service people who were in New York for a meeting. Normally, I would have loved to meet them, but why today?

Bill T told me to check with John from the Financial

Department about Korvette's, but after sitting at that crazy meeting for four hours, I wanted credit for being there so I wrote the story, luckily got the boutique information from the copy overset, and had fifteen minutes of peace before going home.

Friday, February 26

The chairman of Spartans Industries was right: We do print lies. Only it's not our fault. In my page 2 story on yesterday's meeting, I had written that the company was "now making money on its import-contracting business." It came out "not making money..."

My copy was clear and I complained to everyone. Bill T told me I shouldn't use "now." A big correction will run Monday with a head like "Importing Profitable for Spartans." But the mistake is there.

Tuesday, March 2

We had morning and afternoon meetings with John Fairchild about the new medical plan. In my session (afternoon), he looked for people to cite for *DNR*'s success and saw Herb. "You're here again, Herbie?" he asked. (He always calls Herb, "Herbie.")

Only Jerry asked many questions at my meeting. (We were mostly younger staff and girls.) John Fairchild kept dragging out the conversation and then spoke of other things: *W*, the experimental magazine for women, currently being tested on "happy little virgins," the presses, which were just sold to some Tennessee guy. ("When he moves them out, the building may collapse"), and negotiations for an automobile paper, which he would convert to our style of publications. ("Those poor auto people," Gerry said later.)

Wednesday, March 3

John cleaned out his desk (or at least made the attempt) and gave me a brochure for a shoe show. "Guard this," he said. It seems we're going to cover men's shoes—something John has been fighting to do for a long time. I may interview specialty store guys about shoes.

Howard recounted a great Herb story: A former reporter was sent to interview an expensive suit producer. When the *DNR* man got there, the guy showed him a list of statements Herb had written for him to be quoted as saying. After the story ran, Herb was seen wearing his new suit by this manufacturer. After all, he needed suits for his shirts and ties.

Monday, March 8

Only an hour in the office today before John and I went to the shoe show—enough time to see that the page 1 cut's name was spelled wrong and an ad had been sold on my retailing page, reducing the story.

The shoe show was a real pain. We went to the New Yorker in the morning, the Empire State Building and another building in the afternoon, and still didn't hit all the territory. You need a new pair of shoes after that show.

One thing about the manufacturers—they seemed much nicer than men's wear people. Of course they've got a lot to gain if we give them free publicity to clothing people. I wonder what *Footwear News* [Fairchild weekly] will say to all this.

Tuesday, March 9

Van Smith, the artist, asked to borrow my compact. "Why?" I asked.

"To draw my mouth," he said.

[Van Smith gained fame as a costume designer and makeup artist for all of John Waters' films from 1972-2004. During that time, he created the face of drag queen actor, Divine, whose makeup has been described as a cross between Jayne Mansfield and Clarabell the clown. Here, Van was already practicing his makeup skills.]

Rich went to the Ali-Frazier fight last night for fashion pictures and said security was non-existent. He talked to the Kennedys and other celebrities and has the photos to prove it.

At the apparel/retail staff meeting this afternoon, we had an invited guest: Clara. She did a monologue about European fashion that must have lasted a half hour. Like usual, she gave everybody a headache. Howard kept punctuating Clara's talk with funny comments that made me laugh out loud and Clara got upset, saying we weren't taking the meeting seriously enough. (This was at 5:30.)

Walking to the subway with Bill T, he said when he first came to *DNR* as a copy boy, he sometimes worked long hours, like 8 am to 8 pm. But no matter how early he came in or how late he left, Clara was always there before and after. I guess that's why those of us who don't spend 24 hours a day thinking of men's wear find her so hard to take.

Wednesday, March 10

Interesting afternoon discussion with John, Bill T, Peggy, and Van (who gravitates to John although they have nothing in common). John said he wants to go to Copenhagen because of the legalized pornography.

Van tried to convince John that he could see the same stuff in New York. Van lives in the west 40s between 9th and 10th Avenue. Everyone asked him how he could live there.

"It's very safe," he said. "Just a few prostitutes and porno movies being made across the street." He added that if people want to visit him, they should avoid going via the garment district because "that's where people get killed." I guess you need a roadmap.

Memo from Herb to Howard today: "The paper is pink/The story is blue/You write beautifully/I love you."

It was a reference to Howard's Blue Bell 6-7, which had pink color.

Reaction from *Footwear News* to my page 1 shoe story today was nil. John saw Don, who covers men's shoes for *Footwear News*, in a bookstore and Don avoided him, even though they know each other well. (Don once had my job at *DNR*.)

A number of great typos in today's Retailing column: "Tuskaloose" and "Boys went fashion just like their beds" were among the best. My guess is [Alabama stringer] Kathleen's typewriter has a crummy "a" that transmits as an "e."

Thursday, March 11

Van Smith gave two weeks notice.

My byline in today's Retail Sell came out "Berlinger." That's the first time they've spelled it wrong.

I felt very powerful today. I called the head of Wallach's and was told he wasn't available (naturally). But then I told them I might have to run a derogatory story if I couldn't reach him or an exec. Fifteen minutes later, he called me, gave me the information, and practically begged me not to run the BTL (on Wallach's dumping merchandise in the St. George Hotel). We're not going to run it—and I hope he remembers that.

Friday, March 12

Van Smith wore a sequin-studded vest today. Too bad he's leaving.

Kevin heard from *WWD* that Princess Margaret was dead, which sounded strange, especially since yesterday *WWD* said fifteen people were killed on the IRT subway. (It turned out that three people were killed in the I.R.A.) On the radio, the lead story was the premier of Turkey had resigned. Some "senile relative" of a *WWD* staffer had given them the Princess Margaret tip. I hope that's not the usual "reliable source."

Monday, March 15

WWD is unbelievable. Last week they had a "page 1 flash" that minis were back. Today the lead story was "hotskirts" are back. What are "hotskirts"? They look a lot like minis.

Tuesday, March 16

Someone called us about a fire in Gimbels. I phoned their PR department and a girl underling said it was just a little fire that the store put out in two minutes. I was going to take her word until Peggy suggested I check with the fire department—and I'm glad I did. The department said the fire wasn't so small (five pieces of equipment) and the firefighters were still there.

So Sal [photographer] and I rushed to Gimbels, where we smelled the smoke, which was in the basement's ventilation system. The deputy fire chief told me the store hadn't turned in the alarm right away.

Then I called Gimbels again and left a message for Margot, the head PR person. When she called back, I really gave it to her for her incompetent department. She apologized and talked about how hard it is to get good help.

That's twice this week I've been real bitchy to important people. Power!

Wednesday, March 17

Peggy called Dick, who told her when he sees *WWD* photographers at chic restaurants, he yells, "There's a *Women's Wear Daily* photographer!" causing some to run and others to fix their smiles.

Thursday, March 18

Bill Dwyer complimented me on my Gimbels' fire story. He asked if I just happened to be there. (Sure, I always hang around Gimbels.)

[Bill Dwyer, a handsome man in his mid 30s, was our new group vice president, having succeeded James Brady.]

Monday, March 22

Bill Dwyer ran thru *DNR* at lunchtime rattling off newspaper phrases like "30," "stop the presses," "first graph," etc. Maybe he's been taking lessons.

Tuesday, March 23

Peggy saw Amy of *Men's Wear* at the NAMSB [National Association of Men's Sportswear Buyers] show and heard her suggest to a manufacturer that he start a line of boutique maternity clothes. "I'd get pregnant for that," Amy said.

A girl who wants to work at *DNR* (who Mary calls "the young Clara" because of her loud voice) was back again, waiting for Herb.

[Mary, Herb's secretary, was an unmarried middle-aged woman who jumped whenever Herb spoke her name. "Yes, Herb!" she would call as she ran to his side, her blonde pageboy bouncing.]

Thursday, March 25

John gave me advance notice that everyone (including Kevin) was going to be on the Sunday schedule. It's only fair and it just means coming in once every three months.

Friday, March 26

For his last day, Van Smith wore his sequined shirt—"the vulgar Betty Grable look," John called it. Van wore a corsage too.

Monday, March 29

We discussed the "Jewish Princess" article in *New York Magazine* by former *DNR* staffer, Julie Baumgold, and Gerry said it reminded him of Hope [who left *DNR* soon after I started]. Mary agreed and mentioned the times Hope called to say she would be late and asked her to "reserve" a bagel from the coffee man.

Tuesday, March 30

When Sandy and Herb are away, the staff will play. In the afternoon, Kathie, Gerry, and I rummaged through the Great Moments of Journalism file, picking out our favorite items.

Eavesdroppers reported Herb planning lunch with Buffy — and she told him to find a restaurant that allowed hot pants.

[For more about Buffy, *DNR*'s former fashion editor, see "Barney's, Buffy, Ralph, and Me," p. 139]

Wednesday, March 31

Sandy (on vacation) sent John a wire that "the life style shop is becoming a hot retailing concept." He told John to send out assignments about it "right away" and pointed to two recent page 1 stories on "life style."

The only problem is that no one understands "life style." Even after reading the story in today's *DNR* (unsigned, but obviously Sandy's), all I understood is that it's a new-old phrase to describe a not-so-new idea. Life style = shop concept.

I'm just afraid I'll feel like an idiot when I call retailers to ask them about "life style" shops. They won't know what it is and I can't really explain it.

Thursday, April 1

Jerry started picking on me again. It's been a while. He complained about the way I edited a page 1 feature story because I didn't indicate capitals. (I told him I never indicate capitals.)

Friday, April 2

I talked Rich into letting me do a fashion story on the Mets opening day on Tuesday. It wasn't hard since Rich hates baseball. I wrote to the Mets asking for permission for two editors and two photographers to go on the field.

Monday, April 5

I got flowers (beautiful daisies in a basket I could take home) for the second time in my *DNR* career. (The first time was last year on my birthday for a 6-7.) These flowers were for last week's Retail Sell.

Steffi from *WWD* (formerly from *DNR*) is a real Jewish princess. She asked Mary how much comp time she has from *DNR* (she left two years ago). Mary said she no longer keeps the books and Dee doesn't even know Steffi. Then Steffi went to Herb and Personnel, claiming she has five days coming to her, which no one believes. But she must have won her argument because she came back and gave Herb a big kiss.

Someone mentioned Paul of *WWD*, so I told my story about him. We had been on an interview together and took the subway back to the office. Before getting into the 34th Street station, Paul stopped to sign an "End the [Vietnam] War" petition, which I signed too.

A little old lady stood near the petition arguing the hawk point of view. Paul screamed at her in a booming voice, saying she was killing soldiers. He scared the old lady (and me) so much that she tripped going into the subway.

Paul pulled me away and we went into another subway entrance. All the while, he kept asking, "I didn't make her fall did I?" and "It wasn't my fault, was it?"

I half-heartedly tried to reassure him, but we both knew it

was his fault.

It looks good for tomorrow at Shea Stadium. Let's go Mets!

Tuesday, April 6

What a day at Shea! Ki of *WWD*, Sal, and I took a cab to the stadium and got there about noon. I walked around with Sal trying to find well-dressed men to photograph, but there weren't any because it was cold, rainy, and windy.

Ki had Sal take pictures of Beautiful People attending Met owner Joan Payson's party. Afterwards, we went on the field, which our press passes allowed. It was fun, but freezing, and Ki and I sat in the Mets' dugout drinking hot bouillon. The Mets weren't there at the time; they were downstairs in their nice warm clubhouse. Jerry Grote [Mets catcher] came up and yelled at the crowd, "All you crazy people, go home!"

We also saw Lindsay Nelson [announcer], Jerry Koosman [Mets pitcher], Gil Hodges [Mets manager], and Yogi Berra. (There's a picture showing Ki and me on the bench with Yogi in front.) Others we saw: Bob Murphy [announcer], Art Shamsky [Mets outfielder], and Howard Cosell [sports journalist].

It was lots of fun until this old man suddenly said, "No girls in the dugout." Since nothing was happening, we left, Ki to go back to the office since *WWD* was running her story tomorrow, and I was going to go back too because I thought the game would be cancelled.

But when we got outside, it was hardly raining so I decided to stick around. Sal took more pictures and when we heard a cheer, I knew they had taken off the tarp. We returned to the playing field, but this time they refused to let me stay. All of a sudden, it was "no women allowed."

I showed them my pass, which clearly stated I *was* allowed. They couldn't understand it and said I had to clear my pass with management. I pointed out it had been cleared with Mets management: Harold Weissman, head of PR, had signed it.

They conceded I could stay on the field—but only in the corner by the entrance gate near home plate. So, freezing to death, I stood in the drizzle (I wasn't going to leave the field no matter what) and watched the pitchers warm up, saw the color guard walk on, looked at the Channel 9 camera nearby, and watched Sal and the other photographers take pictures.

Then Sal and I went upstairs to the press level to watch the game. However, in the enclosed area, another official told me, "No women allowed in the press section." I was getting very angry.

We sat with the photographers. It was not enclosed, just sheltered. The game was stopped by rain after 4 1/2 innings, with the Mets ahead 4-2. I wanted to go home, but one of the photographers suggested I go to the Press Room for free refreshments. Since all I had eaten was a frank, I wanted to go, but figured I would probably be thrown out because I was a girl. I was right.

I called in a quick BTL to *DNR* since I'm working on the 6-7 for Thursday. But I also called in an "Eye" for *WWD* on the anti-women thing. I titled it, "Women's Lib Take Notice" and explained the discriminatory practices I had come across as a woman reporter. I really hope they use it.

Wednesday, April 7

WWD didn't use my Eye. The editor was very snotty, telling Dee he didn't need *DNR*'s stuff when *WWD* had a reporter at the game. I should have asked Dee to give it to Ki.

When I told Ki what happened, she wanted to do an Eye and Michael, [managing editor] was all for it, providing we got comments from the Mets' and Yankee's front offices and the Baseball Writers Association. But by then, it was too late to reach anyone.

I spent all day working on the 6-7 layout—not the Women's Lib stuff. Another funny thing about Tuesday: I saw a picture of Harold Weissman in the Mets' yearbook and he was one of the guys who yelled at me to get out of the press area and out of the dugout.

Thursday, April 8

Three crazy happenings in *DNR* today:

1. Howard is leaving us. He's going to *Gentleman's Quarterly* where he should have more chance for creativity. All the paeans' reactions were the same: happy and sad. Happy for Howard, but sad for us to lose him around the office.

2. I am being referred to as Susan "Women's Lib" Berliner. I called up the Mets to find out why I wasn't allowed on the field and wound up in a heated argument with PR guy Harold Weissman. After various insults, he told me that there was a "rule" of no women on the field. He implied it was a commission rule and suggested I call a guy at the Commissioner's office. When I did, a minor executive told me (off the record) that there was no such rule. He told me I should write a letter to Joe Reichler, (the man Weissman referred me to). I did that and had Dee type the letter.

When I was in the middle of the Weissman argument, Bill Dwyer handed me a nice note, thanking me for the Mets' 6-7 (which came out fine, so I can use it to prove what I was trying to do at Shea). Bill Dwyer also said in the note that he had written a letter to Mets' owner, Joan Payson.

I showed the Dwyer note to Herb. "I'm going to write one too," Herb immediately said.

Afterwards, I called the Yankee's front office for an opinion on the no-women-on-field rule. The assistant PR guy said there was no such rule and indicated I would be welcome there.

Maybe I should become a Yankee fan.

Total result: three letters, two to Mrs. Payson. I'm sure Herb's was more indignant—praising my work and criticizing the Mets for treating me "like a little girl." (I heard Herb dictating to Mary.) In my letter, I stated my case (with some subtle digs at Weissman). I enclosed the 6-7 and Herb sent Mrs. Payson today's *DNR*.

I figure after all this, I'm either going to be permanently banned from Shea as a reporter or given a season's pass for my suffering. I'd much prefer the latter.

3. I also had an episode with the FBI. I got a call this morning from a man representing Pierre Cardin Neckwear. I had written a retailing story in today's paper in which I quoted a discount chain as selling Cardin ties very cheap.

It turned out the ties sold to the chain had been stolen and the man on the phone wanted me to print that the chain had sold stolen Cardin neckwear.

When I told John, he said since the FBI was investigating, not to do anything. When the guy called back in the afternoon asking what we were going to print, I asked Herb. (John wasn't around and I was having a good day with Herb.)

Herb said we couldn't say the merchandise was stolen and we could only print a statement from the man. I wrote, "A Clarification," saying that Pierre Cardin never sold anything to the discount chain.

Friday, April 9

Herb's daughter, Laurie, visited Daddy. She wore hotpants, but on her they were just shorts. Herb went to lunch with Laurie and then went to the Knicks' playoff game. I wonder if he used comp time.

I was Jerry in the afternoon, doing the BTLs.

Monday, April 12

I made the mistake of asking Jerry how the BTL page turned out and he told me I should've sent through a "timely" BTL, which hadn't looked timely to me. Next time I won't ask.

The word around the office is that Pat, our girl in L.A., whom Sandy was going to "shape up," has shipped out. She quit to reunite with her husband whom she was supposed to have divorced.

I overheard Herb's discussion with Sandy this morning. Herb complained that his good friend (a fashion guy at *GQ*) should have consulted him before hiring Howard to make sure *DNR* could spare him, kind of like a baseball trade.

Tuesday, April 13

Gerry had a Gant interview, with Herb going along, and purposely wore a competitor's shirt.

"I see you're both wearing Gant shirts," the guy said.

"No," Gerry replied.

We asked Gerry if he got some shirts. "No," he said. "But they took Herb's measurements."

John and I glanced through the comp-time book. Kevin's got nine days. How, no one can quite understand.

Wednesday, April 14

Peggy overheard Herb and Sandy talking as if the young Clara had been hired.

Friday, April 16

I had an "executive" lunch with John and Bill T and listened to a lot of complaints about Herb.

"It's like in Bouton's book [*Ball Four*]," Bill said. "When the coach tells the pitcher to throw a guy curves, then when the pitcher throws the batter the curve and it's hit, the coach says, 'I told you not to throw curves.'"

I also discovered what Bill does when he's short of copy: He steals stories that Washington does for our *Pontiac Press* cousins. That's why today's paper had a story about the plights of Indians.

Gerry and Herb both got shirts today, only Herb's box was three times the size of Gerry's.

Tuesday, April 20

The baseball commission's office called me back and Monte Irvin [Hall of Fame former player] told me I'd written a "fine" story on the Mets. I told him it had been difficult to write because I couldn't get on the field.

"Don't worry," Irvin said. "We'll make it possible for you." He said Reichler would call me tomorrow. Everyone in the office thinks I'll get a season's pass.

Wednesday, April 21

I'm still waiting for Reichler's call.

Thursday, April 22

This morning featured the return appearance of the young Clara. She talked to Herb and then left with Sandy.

We had a farewell luncheon for Howard at 68. Herb didn't come. Sandy did, but that didn't deter the luncheon. Howard performed "Mad Dogs and Englishmen" for the last time.

The party atmosphere continued in the afternoon. Fred did his cackling imitation of Clara and Henry, the artist, did his walking imitation of her.

Friday, April 23

Big news today. We crack reporters have just figured out that Gerry and Kathie are getting married. We spent the whole day discussing the rumors and evaluating the evidence. We're all convinced it's true.

Peggy started it off when a woman called for Kathie.

"I'm sorry," Peggy said. "She's on vacation."

"Isn't she getting married tomorrow?" the woman asked.

Other evidence: Dee got a recent call for Kathie from someone who said the apartment was available and she could sign the lease; Kathie is selling her car because (she told Dee), she doesn't need it; and Kathie and Gerry are taking four-week vacations at the same time.

Kathie said she's going to Spain and Portugal with "a close friend" and Gerry said he's going to relax with nothing planned. However, Gerry got photos for an International Driver's License. (Kevin picked up the call that the photos were ready.)

Also, yesterday when John told me why he was against hiring the new Clara, he said, "there are too many pregnable girls around the office: you, Kathie, and Peggy."

"Kathie?" I said. "She's not even married."

John changed the subject and I wasn't suspicious then. We all feel that if we're right, John must know about it because he had to give Gerry and Kathie permission to take their vacations together.

Although Kathie left for "vacation" yesterday, Gerry was still finishing his work. At about 12:30, Peggy, Dee, and I semi-confronted him as he sat at his desk eating lunch. He looked up at us with very frightened eyes.

"Where are you going on your vacation?" Peggy asked.

"Why do you want to know?" Gerry replied.

"We just want to know," Peggy said.

Then we realized how unfair we were being and apologized to him.

Gerry finally left at 4:30 and although John was off today, I wanted to talk to him about this (and Bill T had a *DNR* question) so I called. Our discussion went like this:

Me: "John, the whole office is buzzing: Are Gerry and

Kathie getting married?"

John: "Why do you ask?"

I began listing our reasons. Howard and Peggy, who hovered over me, picked up the phone to fill in points I left out.

John: "That's interesting, but I can't tell you anything about it."

Me: "But John, it's over the whole office. We've been talking about it all day."

John: "Who knows about it?"

Me: "Just about everybody."

John: "Well, let me put it this way. If it were true, don't you think they would have a reason for not telling anyone?"

Me (flabbergasted): "What reason?"

John: "Maybe there's a company policy. Please try to keep it quiet."

Peggy, Howard, and I, on extensions, looked at each other. Sandy knows, but at least Herb doesn't. Sandy got on the phone and John said something to him. (I imagine it was, "Yes, it's true, but I'll explain Monday.")

Then John must have asked if there were people around him because Sandy said, "Yes, there's a crowd here."

Afterwards, I asked Bill T if there is a company policy prohibiting intra-company marriages. He said, "No." I'll have to ask John about this on Sunday when we work together.

Other happenings: I called the Baseball Commissioner's office, but no one was in. Monday I really must start with the Human Rights Commission. Sandy said I could interview Frank Gifford because he's moved to ABC Sports [to broadcast Monday Night Football].

Sunday, April 25

My first Sunday in the office was strange. It was dark and deserted, with only John, two proofreaders, the copy boy, and me. I didn't have to wait long to find out how we'd get around to talking about Kathie and Gerry. Before I removed my coat, John said, "So tell me about Friday."

I told him, repeating all the clues. He never admitted anything, always prefacing his responses with, "If it were true..." But he didn't deny anything either.

I read the *Times*' wedding articles—no mention of them. Then Howard called with a new piece of information: Jerry's passport photo. I was in the office from 10:15 to 3:45, but did very little work. I edited one story, looked through the *Times* for news items we could have missed, and sent through three BTLs.

My major contribution was organizing the Great Moments of Journalism into categories. I came up with Great Industry Faces, Great Fashion Moments, Great PR Releases, Great Inter-Office Memos, Great Letters, and Great Published (or Almost Published) Moments. Everything fit into a category.

Monday, April 26

We didn't give up our research on Kathie and Gerry. New evidence: Kathie's had written in her calendar on a page in early April, "Dresses should be in" and the page for Saturday, April 24 had three stars (***).

One funny incident: Long ago, someone told Rich that Gerry was married with two kids so he thought Gerry was having an affair with Kathie. "It was more exciting that way," Rich said.

Howard felt he'd been used as a "front." Gerry and Kathie always walked to the west side together, but recently they asked Howard to come with them. Gerry would stop at Sixth Avenue and Howard walked Kathie to the Seventh Avenue subway.

Tuesday, April 27

The young Clara has been hired. John told me in the morning and I asked when she was starting.

"In a week or two," John said.

I couldn't believe it. Howard has stayed an extra week to help train his replacement.

Late in the day, Peggy and I asked Kevin why he told Herb about Kathie and Gerry. Kevin said Herb had heard Peggy's initial outburst, therefore it was all right for him (Kevin) to ask Herb, "Have you heard about Kathie?"

"Why bring it up?" we asked.

Kevin argued that the company wouldn't do anything about it because it would be a long, expensive court case. But who is he to decide?

Wednesday, April 28

John was in an especially lousy mood because Kevin had gone to Personnel to ask if we had a rule prohibiting married couples from working on the same paper. Now John's afraid that when Kathie and Gerry return, they'll both quit.

The Gerry-Kathie situation is already known in the industry. Peggy got a call from a designer who knew about it — and his info sounded like it came from *DNR*.

Peggy collected money for a gift for Howard. We're getting him a gift certificate for Sam Goody's.

Next week what's left of the *DNR* staff will practically all be going to a machinery trade show in Atlantic City. Peggy will be the whole apparel department.

I had lunch with John, Bill T, and Clara, and Clara told us how she and Gail from *WWD* are working on *W*, which is supposed to be a weekly for affluent women. (It's been talked about for five years.) Clara said John Fairchild and James Brady told her and Gail to come up with ideas for the new paper and the two of them stayed up all night thinking of things. But the next day, Brady said, "I've got some great ideas" and Gail and Clara never got to present theirs.

Friday, April 30

It was Howard's last day and he looked like he was crying because of a bad cold and stuffed nose.

A woman from *Supermarket News,* who's a big advocate for Women's Lib, gave me information on the Civil Liberties Union. I called the N.Y.C.L.U. about the Mets and the lawyer's secretary was very interested. I'm going there on Monday.

Monday, May 3

We're even more short-handed than we expected: Bill T's wife is in the hospital with colitis so he'll be out all week.

I brought a copy of my Baseball Commissioner's letter, my pass, and my *DNR* story to the Civil Liberties Union. Toby seemed interested and said a woman lawyer might handle my case.

Tuesday, May 4

More on the Kathie-Gerry story. Matt called from the Knitting Show and said someone there asked him, "Is Gerry married yet? He told me he was getting married." We're all annoyed that industry people know more than we do.

At the end of the day, I made the mistake of asking Jerry to finish editing the page 1 story. I should have waited till tomorrow because I had to stay late and listen to Jerry tell me I should stay home and have babies, I should type in corrections, and I should wait while he finished editing the story.

Wednesday, May 5

Monte Irvin from the Baseball Commissioner's Office called me and explained that all I have to do is call Weissman and I'll get permission to be on the field of Shea Stadium.

"That's fine," I said. "But what about that 'no-women-on-the-field' rule?"

"It was all a mistake," Irvin said.

I told Irvin that if it was a mistake, I want it in writing, plus an apology from Weissman, who, according to Irvin, is "sorry" about what happened. (I don't believe it.) I mentioned I was working with the N.Y.C.L.U. and would continue working with them until I got a satisfactory letter from Weissman or the Commissioner's Office, apologizing and stating that women are allowed on the field.

He said I would get the letter early next week. I thanked him for his help. After all, I have no argument with him. He's been very nice and I'm sure he doesn't like being the middleman.

I phoned the N.Y.C.L.U. after and was told a woman lawyer would call me soon.

Thursday, May 6

I had to work on a news story today: The Amalgamated Clothing Workers complained to the FTC about phony union labels in suits. Since they mentioned Macy's, I called their PR department, all set to tangle with Eleanor, who's almost as bad as Margot from Gimbels. But Eleanor was on vacation and I got a nice underling who listened to the union's release and then cried, "I knew I should have stayed home today!"

On the same story, our Washington bureau (the only one that functions as a bureau — with eight to ten people — because of *Pontiac Press*), got a comment from the FTC, told us the case was being handled in NY, and gave us the lawyer's name and phone number.

When I called and asked to speak to the lawyer, the woman said, "What ship?"

"Is this the FTC?" I asked.

"No," she said. "This is Pier 17."

Our bureau had transposed the first two digits.

Herb left for his month's vacation after lunch. You could feel the relief around the office.

Friday, May 7

It's amazing what the absence of Herb does for *DNR*. I've never seen the staff in such good spirits. But after lunch things got a bit dismal again. Marty, our man in Willingboro has a bleeding ulcer and will be out for at least a week. That means John has to go down to Willingboro, with Al and Sandy perhaps having to go too.

Fairchild got rid of more people, cutting the library research staff by converting the morgue into an "information center." We're just going to have index cards.

My questions: "What happens when you need background for a late-breaking news story? Do you start looking at index cards and flip through microfilm?"

The answer seems to be "yes." The solution: You omit the background.

Monday, May 10

Myrna is our new Howard and she's real gung-ho. One can hardly blame her. This is her first job and it took her four months to get it. I had lunch with her and stopped myself from being too opinionated. She'll find things out for herself. First problem: She likes Herb. He does make a good impression and I like him too—but not as a publisher.

Tuesday, May 11

Lee [proofreader] asked me if a girl my age could fall in love and want to marry a man his age [over 50], putting me on the spot. He said there had been a girl who wanted to marry him. That's really something since, as I told Lee, she'd be getting five children in the deal and he's still got some young kids living at home.

Wednesday, May 12

I had my Frank Gifford interview. He struck me as nice and rather shy. Since he hasn't started on ABC yet, I told Sandy it would be good to run the story soon.

"How about Monday?" he asked.

I didn't mean that soon.

Clara calls Dee, "Deedledee," which annoys Dee, but there's nothing she can do about it. I suggested (if she wants to get fired) calling Clara, "Clarabell." I was rewarded for my idea later in the day by being called "SusieQ."

Thursday, May 13

A hundred percent day, including a PR luncheon, listening to a promotion for the city of Louisville, KY for 2 1/2 hours. But I got a nice meal at Le Pavillon.

I also finished the Gifford story, except for the final editing.

Monday, May 17

I'm working at the Boutique Show with Rich on Sunday. John asked me, and since Kathie and Gerry are still out, I'm the logical one, with Myrna being so new.

Tuesday, May 18

I had to cover a boring J.C. Penney annual meeting today because John had another meeting to go to. I met a new girl for *HFD* there who came to Fairchild from the *Chicago Tribune* where she was a general reporter. She became a reporter right out of college because they have no newspaper guild. In New York, a job like that is impossible.

Back in the office, everyone was laughing about this typo

in a BTL about smog in Tokyo: "Fanned by high rise in temperature, combination of factory smoke and auto exhaust fumes created health hazard nearly two months earlier than in '70 when 30 schoolgirls were felled by cock choking skoke."

Wednesday, May 19

Two people are leaving Fairchild, one voluntarily and one involuntarily. The voluntary one is Michael, the artist, and to that I say, "good riddance."

The other is Frank, head of FNS (Fairchild News Service), a shock because he's been here all his working life—over fifteen years—and he's competent, reliable, and easy to get along with. I went to Frank whenever I sent assignments to correspondents (stringers).

Myrna showed us she'd already developed gray hairs after only a week at *DNR*. John produced his inheritance from Howard: some of Howard's last-pulled white hairs. John always said Howard was knitting a yarmulke.

Thursday, May 20

Steffi was named *WWD*'s London correspondent. My reaction was "good," one less arrogant person. John and Bill T were offended. They think she's just quiet. Mary Lois and Peggy agreed with me, but said Steffi's not a girl's girl.

I met Howard getting out of the train today. He's a bit disillusioned with the *GQ* job. He did an exposé of the magazine, which was read to the staff, obviously creating friction. However, Howard did have lunch with Sammy Davis, Jr. Also, he cheered up reading the anti-static story in *DNR*, knowing he didn't have to write it.

Friday, May 21

Cleanup day for our move. We put our belongings into cartons and after lunch, Peggy and I went up to the fourth floor to look at our new quarters. There was an office and conference room for Bill Dwyer, but no office for Herb. The only other enclosed area was around the air-conditioning apparatus. Harry and Frank S of our textiles department, who were up at the same time, suggested Herb could fit in there.

At least this place is bright and cheerful, much better than our "Front Page"-looking third floor firetrap with its tilted floors and bugs. (Earlier this week, we spotted a gigantic cockroach near John Fairchild's office. It was so big that no one would crush it.)

Monday morning will be fun. Nobody knows where they are sitting and Kathie and Gerry are returning. But I'm working Sunday so I'll get a sneak preview.

Sunday, May 23

This was a real working Sunday—roaming the corridors of the McAlpin for two hours at the Boutique Show and then meeting Rich for lunch.

During lunch, Mike, our Philly ad man, came over to tell us he'd brought his wife and daughter to the show. That's kind of a strange way to spend a Sunday, but he's kind of strange—the guy who carries an oar in his car to act out his aggressions. While he was talking, I kept thinking about the oar and hoping he wouldn't get angry with us.

Back at the office to write my story, I got a look at our new seating setup. Bill T and Sandy are far removed from everyone and we don't face them. I always thought the news desk belonged in the center of things.

Monday, May 24

Kathie and Gerry came back today and, after talking about them for four weeks, I managed to miss their entrance because my subway train was thirty minutes late.

When I finally rushed in, John tried to convince me the rumors were wrong. Pulling me aside, he said, "I think you're going to be surprised when you speak to Gerry and Kathie."

"Huh?" I said. But then I looked at Kathie, saw her engagement ring and wedding band, and knew we had been right. Later, everyone rehashed the rumors and clues with the happy couple, who enjoyed hearing about them now that everything was over. Besides, they'd been well informed on company gossip by John at their breakfast "briefing."

Today was also moving day and we had a fair amount of gripes. I sit near the air conditioning apparatus and it was turned on and freezing. The phones were crazy because we're in new seats with our old extensions.

Tuesday, May 25

I'm collecting for a party for Gerry and Kathie. We're having it in Kevin's house again since he was kind enough to suggest it. I'm asking for $6 because, after all, there are two of them and they shouldn't be cheated out of a present because they married each other.

We're having the party next Wednesday, June 2. Unfortunately, John will be on vacation in North Carolina and Bill T will be off too. It's vacation time so it would be impossible to get everyone.

Rich asked if we should buy Michael a gift.

"He should buy us a gift for tolerating him," I said.

Wednesday, May 26

Gerry reminded me this morning that I had been promoted. It took me a minute to remember that Sandy had authorized me to be the temperature checker to deal with the air conditioning. We decided my new title is "Environmental Control Specialist."

Late in the afternoon, I got a chance to test my new

authority. However, my authority went unrecognized: The temperature was not changed.

Tuesday, June 1

Peggy and I went to the bank to get a gift check of $120 for Gerry and Kathie. Rich bought the liquor. Tomorrow we'll shop for groceries.

It's still freezing up here. I think I'm going to give Mary my Environmental Control Specialist job. I called once and got the air conditioner turned off. But after lunch, they turned it on again. When I called, nothing happened. I asked Mary to call and two minutes later, a man shut the air conditioning off.

Wednesday, June 2

The party for Kathie and Gerry turned out quite well, but without the liveliness of Peggy's party last December [to celebrate her marriage]. One reason for the quieter atmosphere was the absence of John, Bill T, and Al. But Howard came. He's much happier at GQ now, interviewing Johnny Carson next week. Sandy came too, but couldn't fit into any conversation and left early. Bill Dwyer, on the other hand, mingled well and stayed late, leaving when I did (7:30). Kathie and Gerry were pleased with the gift (cleverly wrapped in a tie box by Peggy).

Great typo in today's New York Times: "It [Tricia Nixon's wedding cake] will have the initials of the President's daughter and her bridegroom, Edward Finch Cox, and will be iced in white, decorated with blown Cox and will be iced in sugar lovebirds, white roses and pink-tinged cherry blossoms."

Friday, June 4

Today's big question: Who stole Clara's copies of W. Five sample copies of WWD's experimental weekly for rich women were left on Clara's desk in the morning. Since they were on her desk and stood out (the cover featured caricatures of the

Nixons), everyone borrowed the copies, including me. I returned mine, but others didn't. At the end of the day, none of the copies remained, only a note that read, "See what you think."

Dee tried to round up some of the missing copies and I helped her, but no luck. When Dee called *WWD* for more copies, she couldn't get any. James Brady was horrified that other people had seen the paper. It was not meant for our eyes.

Tuesday, June 8

I'm back in action against the Mets. I called Nancy, the lady lawyer, and she was very nice, apologizing for not calling me earlier and agreeing to write a letter to Harold Weissman (carbon to the Baseball Commission) on Civil Liberties' stationery.

Wednesday, June 9

At lunch with Kathie, Gerry, and Peggy, we asked *WWD*'s Tricia who's taking over for Steffi. She said Rosemary, with Daphne Davis taking Rosemary's market.

The name rang a bell. "Isn't she the girl from *Rags* magazine?" I asked.

"Yes," Tricia said.

Daphne Davis was on David Frost's TV show with John Fairchild—she with her jeans and he with his distinguished appearance. All she did was criticize *WWD* for forcing women to wear what it wanted them to and now she's working for *WWD*. I guess she would rationalize it by saying she's working to better *WWD* from the inside.

Thursday, June 10

WWD's lead Eye story today: *Rags* is going out of business. I wonder who gave them that information.

Gerry came back in late afternoon with a batch of free shirts and ties. But I did better: Larry got a free suit, sports jacket and knit slacks from my only generous retailer.

Friday, June 11

Ginny in Philly had written me a note asking, "Who is Myrna????"

"Myrna is Howard," I answered.

Later in the day (on suggestion of Bill B), Myrna wrote: "Yes, Virginia, there is a Myrna."

Wednesday, June 16

Bill Dwyer motioned me into his new office to ask my advice on how he should arrange the furniture. I was flattered, but felt funny offering suggestions. I did tell him I would move the dresser-type piece to another wall and he did that later.

Clara stuck me with a phone call from her friend Sy, head of the NAMSB [National Association of Men's Sportswear Buyers]. One of the retailers I interviewed last month at the Boutique Show claims I misquoted him and wrote letters to Clara and Herb (not me, of course).

I told Sy I didn't misquote the guy and that I had my notes to prove it. (I later checked and surprisingly *did* still have my notes.) We talked for thirty minutes with nothing decided. I'm not printing a retraction. It's not my fault the guy got in trouble by saying the NAMSB was unnecessary.

Thursday, June 17

Clara brought up yesterday's phone call so I told her what happened. She was shocked I hadn't heard about the incident before, but claimed the guy never wrote to her. Clara said she told Sy I was too good a reporter to misquote the guy. I never knew Clara thought so highly of me.

Myrna got her first disillusionment today. She met a nasty PR woman who ruined her afternoon.

Jerry finally returned from vacation, walking into the office at 5:15. His first word: "Goddamnit!"

Friday, June 18

After Myrna's depressing day yesterday, we decided she was ready for a brief introduction to the Great Moments file. I started her off on Great Industry Faces. Her response was very good. Maybe we'll show her Great Fashion Moments next.

Wednesday, June 23

Rich, Kathie, Mary Lois, and I spent part of the afternoon thinking of a head for a Madras 6-7. My favorite: "Once Upon a Madras."

Jerry yelled at me for my sloppy copy on the Wall Street 6-7. I argued that I typed in corrections. He said there were too many corrections. You can't win.

Thursday, June 24

They're running my 6-7 tomorrow—talk about last-minute decisions. Poor Fred had to do it at lunchtime.

Friday, June 25

We showed Myrna Great Fashion Moments and Great Cards and Letters.

My 6-7 ran without typos, rather unusual.

Tuesday, June 29

It was almost a horrible day. When I walked into the office, John told me Herb wanted a reaction story from retailers on Frank's Monday article about knit fabric standards. I wasn't happy about this because: (1) I didn't understand Frank's story (2) I didn't see how retailers would understand the technical points (3) I didn't see how I could explain the story to retailers since manufacturers didn't understand it (4) I didn't see how it was worth a story and (5) I didn't want to explain the story to our correspondents, who often don't have a recent copy of *DNR*.

But when I reread the story, I realized knit standards had nothing to do with performance, which made a retailing story worthless. After all, the only thing that concerns retailers is customer reaction, e.g. performance.

I told this to John, who asked Frank, who agreed it wasn't for retailers. Then John talked to Sandy, who checked with Herb, who called off the story. Herb just wants a story in the near future on how retailers view knit products.

Two PR guys for a Houston department store took John and me to lunch. The meal at The Homestead was delicious.

Mary Lois had copies of an old Fairchild men's magazine on London fashion. It was amazing how many of the 1927 styles, fabrics, and motifs fit into today's men's wear picture.

Thursday, July 1

Van Smith stopped by and at first no one recognized him. He had a neat goatee and short hair. But Van still looked different: He wore no shoes.

Wednesday, July 7

I had to check the union pickets at Klein's. It turned out to be only five old men in front of the store. The spokesman said there were fifteen picketers, but many were out for lunch. This was about noon, when all the shoppers come and the union guys were supposed to be "educating" the public about imports. But Bill T was short on page 1 stories and needed this.

Then after lunch, Bill T got a tip from the union that Klein's had agreed not to import any more suits. But Klein's avoided us the rest of the afternoon and Bill couldn't reach the union so we just ran the picketing story.

Thursday, July 8

Short apparel meeting discussing complaints against Jerry for not letting anyone know what he's doing. Result: Duplication of material in the paper, making us look stupid.

Friday, July 9

Herb had wanted me to go to Louis Armstrong's funeral yesterday. (Why? Because I live in Queens.) But I protested that I couldn't identify the celebrities attending and suggested Fred go. Unbelievably, Herb let Fred go—and he was able to identify all the attendees.

Monday, July 12

I made what Bill T kiddingly called the "worst newspaper mistake" possible: I pasted my two Tuesday retailing pages (13 and 14) together as a double-page layout. The only trouble is pages 13 and 14 aren't across from one another—14 is behind 13. The plant called Bill, hysterical about it. At least they weren't mad.

Tuesday, July 13

Julie Baumgold came to Fairchild to research men's high-heeled shoes for a *New York Magazine* story. She wore a long see-through checkered dress and said she'd never been a Jewish princess.

Wednesday, July 14

More union problems, with Klein's signing a contract with the ACW [Amalgamated Clothing Workers]. According to Bill T, I just had to call Klein's for verification on the union's press release. But it wasn't that easy because Klein's again ignored my calls. Finally, the union called Klein's to tell them to talk to us.

A few hours later, the Klein's guy I tried to call last week phoned me, half-apologizing. Only trouble was, he didn't agree with the union's statement, which said Klein's agreed not to import any more men's and boys' clothing. He said boys' clothing was never mentioned.

When I called the union's PR guy, his comment was, "Oy."

Finally, I got both statements and wrote the story.

Thursday, July 15

James Brady resigned as publisher of *WWD*. He's going to Hearst Publications. John Fairchild was named publisher to go with his chairmanship.

Friday, July 16

Kathie, Gerry, Mary Lois, and I met Howard for lunch. Howard brought the *New York Times*' story on Brady's resignation. John Fairchild's quote on Brady: "He's so terrific."

At lunch, Mary Lois revealed she'll be doing BTLs most of the time from now on, replacing Jerry, who'll become a "floating reporter." I wonder if this is a voluntary abdication on Jerry's part to concentrate on features.

Sunday, July 18

I had to work with Jerry, so I brought Larry with me for comfort. I showed him the Great Moments in Journalism file, but he didn't appreciate it. I guess one has to work here to really appreciate it.

Nothing much happened, but it's lousy spending a Sunday in the office during the summer.

Tuesday, July 20

Another of my good retail sources quit to go to a Minneapolis chain. Every time a guy is willing to quote figures to me, he leaves.

Thursday, July 22

Myrna had a repeat phone confrontation with MacGregor's obnoxious PR woman. Myrna told her how much she resented their first meeting and how embarrassed she had felt. The woman was stunned. She'd thought everything went beautifully. After Myrna hung up, we all congratulated her.

The union began picketing Alexander's so I had to go to the 59th Street store.

Monday, July 26

More union trouble: Macy's agreed to remove non-union labels from imported suits. Unfortunately, however, Macy's and the union didn't exactly agree and I had to dig for information. I'd hoped to work on the Frank McGee [TV newscaster] feature.

Tuesday, July 27

Barney's merchandising manager was named president of Genesco's RAM [Retail Apparel for Men] division. Everyone at *DNR* liked that move because Mel gives us discounts on men's suits and he was hampered at Barney's, not even allowed to give interviews.

While John, who's on vacation, will be happy with the news, I wasn't happy having to do the story because we had no information on Mel's background and Mel was on vacation. Since our morgue files are no longer available, I had to check file cards on microfilm.

Friday, July 30

Pouring rain and flooding, but an easy day. Everyone was drenched and Gerry borrowed dry sample socks from Myrna — red with "sex" written all over.

Kevin was supposed to do BTLs today. (Whoever works Sunday is supposed to do BTLs on Friday), but Sandy, who's on vacation, forgot to tell him, so Kevin refused. When no one volunteered, Kathie said she'd do them.

Monday, August 2

John came back from vacation and Sandy got to him immediately, updating him on all the gossip. But John already knew everything. Was he surprised at Brady's resignation?

"No," he said. "Jerry told me about that rumor weeks ago."

Capital Cities' earnings were up, a good sign.

Tuesday, August 3

The president of Arlan's Department Store resigned soon after a shake-up at the annual meeting. Since Sam of *WWD*, who had done the annual meeting story, was on vacation, I had to call Arlan's. But those people ignore girls.

After I'd written the story (basically rewriting Sam's story, with background), the secretary at Arlan's called me and said the guy had spoken to Dennis of *WWD*, so I should call him. I hate going through *WWD* like that, but it turned out the guy told Dennis nothing. (Dennis probably asked nothing.) As a result, we stuck to my story, which was more informative.

Thursday, August 5

The ACW union decided to stage another protest, which made me panic. I needed today to finish my Frank McGee story before vacation. I suggested sending one of the copy people and luckily John agreed. The protest turned out to be nothing.

In the afternoon, I briefed Peggy on retailing.

Friday, August 6

I finished the McGee story and got most of the dummies out of the way when Kathie announced that the Window Trimmers Union was picketing Bonds. Since I wanted to leave at 1 pm, after I called the union for background, Kathie offered to write the story.

I spent the morning telling everyone, "See you in September."

California, here I come!

[Unfortunately, I never saw my coworkers in September because I returned from that four-week cross-country vacation with a case of mononucleosis. And when I went back to *DNR* in October, I didn't continue the journal. I didn't follow up on my "Women's Lib" issue with the Mets either. Although I never got an apology from the team—let alone free tickets—I'm still a huge Mets fan.]

BARNEY'S, BUFFY, RALPH, AND ME

I had an important *Daily News Record* assignment: interviewing Fred Pressman, head of Barney's, the trendy men's store, for a Page 1 feature story.

When I returned from the interview, muttering about how difficult it had been to extract information from Pressman, Buffy, our fashion editor, asked to see my notes. Figuring she probably planned to do a story on Barney's latest clothing line, I handed her my notepad.

Buffy was an interesting character. Thin and humorless, she wore granny glasses, her hair in a prim bun, and favored midi skirts, the new fashion length that most women hated. Men thought Buffy was hot; I thought she was cold. But she was my coworker so I tried to get along with her.

When I finished writing my Barney's story, I gave it to Jerry, our grumpy features editor, and then promptly forgot about it. Since it wasn't a news article—and Pressman hadn't revealed any earth-shattering information—there was no rush and scheduling Page 1 interviews was entirely up to Jerry.

"Susan, when is your Barney's story going to run?" Buffy asked me about a week later.

"I don't know," I said—and I wasn't going to pester Jerry, who would have hissed at me.

When the interview didn't run during the next few weeks and Buffy questioned me about it again, I just shrugged. Jerry hadn't mentioned anything about it.

About a month after I'd written the Barney's story, I picked up the first edition of *Boutique Magazine*, one of several publications seeking to capitalize on the popularity of the little fashion shops sprouting up throughout Manhattan.

Near the front of the issue was an interview with Fred Pressman, filled with quotes from my story. I showed the magazine to my editor, who took it to our publisher, and later that day, Buffy was fired.

Afterwards, I found out what had happened. Buffy was dating a former salesman for Fairchild Publications, who'd left our trade paper chain to launch *Boutique Magazine*. When she copied my Pressman quotes, Buffy expected *DNR*, a daily newspaper, to publish the feature story long before the new monthly magazine debuted. But, thanks to Jerry, that hadn't happened.

In hindsight, I did Buffy a huge favor. In *DNR*, she had touted the fashions of a new men's wear designer: Ralph Lauren. After being fired, she joined Lauren's young company as his personal assistant, rising to become executive vice-president.

And my Barney's story? It finally ran soon after *Boutique Magazine*'s debut. But by then, it was old news.

———

A few years ago, I discovered Larry's chiropractor had been retained by Ralph Lauren, who flew him around the world to treat the designer's aching back.

"Ask the chiropractor if he knows Buffy," I told my husband.

The answer was he did.

"Have him ask Buffy if she remembers me," I urged.

"Say 'hi' to Susan," was the message the chiropractor relayed.

Of course Buffy remembered me. She could have thanked me too.

A WAKE-UP TALE

One summer afternoon in the early 1970s, I stood on the platform of the 14th Street-Union Square subway station waiting for the uptown IRT local—not an unusual occurrence because I generally took the train to my assignments for *Daily News Record*.

Since it was off-peak hours, the local didn't come quickly so I stood there daydreaming until I heard the engine's roar and saw the train entering the station. That's when I realized I was alone except for the man standing next to me.

He was tall—at least 6-foot 6-inches—Black, with a large bushy beard. He held a staff, was barefoot, and wore only a white loincloth. The man reminded me of a biblical prophet.

After the train stopped and the doors opened, I got on, followed by the tall, bearded, nearly naked man. Although the car was almost empty, when I took a seat in the center, the man sat next to me. The few riders in our section either slithered far away from us or escaped to another compartment.

As the train slowly lumbered uptown, I sat completely still, afraid to disturb the neighboring giant. And whenever the local stopped at a station, people entering our compartment sat along the periphery, far from the two of us, or fled through the sliding doors. Throughout the ride, the man next to me sat silently, clutching his staff, and staring straight ahead.

When we reached 42nd Street/Grand Central Station, the man rose from his seat and exited the train. I don't know where he went—maybe to the nearby library. Or perhaps he took the shuttle to Times Square, which has always featured strange characters, although this was long before costumed Elmos and superheroes took up residence there.

The incident taught me an important lesson: Always pay attention to your surroundings. Now whenever I wait in a public place, I don't daydream because you never know who can materialize next to you.

LADY LEGEND

Clara was one of the first women reporters in the men's wear industry, hired to cover boys' clothing for *Daily News Record* during World War II because few men were available. She stayed with *DNR* for the next fifty years.

When I met Clara, she was already an industry legend, a woman who knew everyone and everything involved in the men's wear business. She was married, but had no children, and devoted her boundless energy to the job.

By then Clara didn't come into the office every day. However, since she wrote a weekly column, she clomped to her desk at least once each week to type it. I use the word "clomped" because that's what this tiny dark-haired dynamo did: Clara clomped, taking short running steps with her high heels banging on the floor.

After making a noisy entrance, Clara usually visited Herb, our publisher, ignoring me, the other young reporters, and even the senior editors.

When Clara left Herb's office, she clomped to her freestanding desk behind me. Clara's desk had nothing on it except a telephone, which she used all the time. And Clara was screechingly loud. Listening to her on the phone in our large open room (no partitions except those forming the publisher's "office") made it difficult for me and everyone else to concentrate.

One day when Clara wasn't at her desk and her phone rang, one of the reporters answered the call. "Look at this!" he yelled afterwards, hoisting the beige receiver in the air for all of us to see.

The inside of the phone was badly corroded. Clara's constant chatter with her mouth pressed against the receiver had eaten away the hard plastic.

Clara might have been an industry legend, but when I think of her, I remember that corroded, disgusting-looking telephone.

FREELANCE PHASE

When my children were little, I worked at home as a full-time mom. However, from the late 1970s through the mid 1980s, I also freelanced as a telephone sales rep, newspaper reporter, and educational writer/editor.

My first freelance job was for Roger and Mary, husband and wife entrepreneurs who sold educational filmstrips and workbooks from their home office in nearby Amawalk and needed a phone rep to solicit sales from school librarians and teachers' stores.

It was a great experience because Roger and Mary were delightful, fair people—even giving me a phone code so my business calls would be billed directly to them—and I was able to work at home in my den, scheduling calls around the children's naps and needs. When Mary and Roger switched businesses—selling nursing videos in the new VCR format—I worked for them again, this time phoning hospitals and nursing schools.

———

In the early 1980s, Mary and Roger introduced me to their neighbor, John, who owned Arden Communications, a magazine publishing company. As a phone rep, I sold display advertising for John's consumer magazines: *Today's Photographer, Modern Trucking,* and several smaller digests.

John's full-size publications were impressive, featuring glossy photos and well-written articles. But all his magazines had one major flaw: They never came out on time. I would tell advertisers the next issue of *Today's Photographer* would be published in February and the magazine would appear in May. My customers hated the inaccurate deadlines and few repeated their ads.

In addition to not publishing his magazines on time, John never had enough funds to pay all his employees. On the rare times John deposited money into Arden's account, his assistant, Brendan, would phone everyone and urge us to rush to John's Mount Kisco bank to cash our checks before funds ran out. (He had moved into the Victorian mansion on Main Street in Mount Kisco known as the "Ragtime house," because the award-winning movie, *Ragtime,* had been filmed there.)

John's sister, Marge, also sold advertising for Arden and she too had trouble extracting money from her brother. When I solicited ads for *Modern Trucking,* Marge paid me in merchandise: a patio table and chairs.

I forgot about John for many years—until he made New York newspaper headlines in 2009. John was arrested in Long Island for harassing Rudy Giuliani, who he claimed drummed up phony tax charges against him as Manhattan district attorney in the early 1980s.

Maybe that's why John never had money.

———

Besides being a sales rep, in the late 1970s and early 1980s I was a freelance reporter for my local weekly newspaper, the *North County News,* covering meetings of Yorktown's town board, planning board, and zoning board.

It was a perfect set-up because all the board meetings were nearby and held at night, allowing Larry to baby-sit while I worked. It also gave me a connection to the *Yorktown PennySaver*, which owned the newspaper, and in 1986 hired me full-time to do the company's promotion.

———

During the 1980s, I also worked at home on many freelance educational writing projects, most of them with Larry. I wrote English textbooks, created reading passages for standardized tests, edited a publication called *Science Weekly*, and created school activity guides for Lifetime Learning Systems, a Connecticut company.

In 1989, Larry got a freelance job, writing questions for Partners in English, a *Reader's Digest* guide for teachers to use with their middle school and high school students. The guide also included puzzles, vocabulary, and activities for students, which I would have loved to create, but another freelance writer retained that assignment.

Then in 1992, *Reader's Digest* abruptly awarded Partners in English to a different company, ending Larry's employment.

"Who's doing the guide now?" my husband asked.

"Oh, you wouldn't know them," his boss said. "It's a Connecticut company called Lifetime Learning Systems."

Larry immediately called Dominic at Lifetime Learning, had a meeting with him, and got us both jobs: Larry would write the discussion questions and activities and I would do the puzzles and vocabulary.

Creating those teachers' guides was a ten-months-a-year project, for which we at first used 21-23 stories, basically every article in each *Reader's Digest* issue.

Working with pre-press galley copies of the stories, Larry and I organized the issues on our living room floor, choosing the best five for activities, vocabulary, and puzzles. I also constructed a full-page vocabulary-based crossword puzzle.

It was a wonderful, though challenging and exhausting, experience. Each month, Larry had to take a day off from teaching middle-school English to finish his part of the (at first) 16-page guide and we both worked like crazy during our one-week timeframe to complete what we called, "the project."

However, as *Reader's Digest* downsized its publication, we downsized the guide too. Here's a timeline:

* 1993: 20-21 stories, 16-page guide
* 1997: 16 stories, still 16-page guide
* 1998: Barbara, our editor at Lifetime Learning, leaves the company. However, she takes the *Reader's Digest* project with her and retains Larry and me to write it. Partners in English now includes just 8 stories in an 8-page guide.
* 2003: 3-5 stories, previously published in *Reader's Digest*, are repackaged into a booklet for students—and we have no control over the chosen articles. Although our teachers' guide remains 8 pages, the guide cover, which had consisted of story titles, now features photos of green-hued kids.

These last changes also meant students no longer received the current edition of *Reader's Digest*—which I thought had been the purpose of this project: to encourage kids to read the magazine.

In May of 2008, *Reader's Digest* ended Partners in English. At that point, it was a mercy killing.

MR. CHASE'S PENNYSAVER

The Yorktown *PennySaver*, founded in 1958 by John Chase and his wife, Christa, was a true mom-and-pop success story. He sold the ads to local businesses and then the two of them mimeographed the pages of the shopper in their Yorktown home's garage.

When I began working full-time for the company in 1986, the *PennySaver* was a thriving enterprise. It consisted of 20 editions in Westchester, Putnam, and Dutchess counties, mailed weekly to 330,000 homes. Our Yorktown headquarters, plus branch offices in Wappingers Falls and Poughkeepsie, handled walk-in traffic and phone calls.

By then, my boss, always outspoken, had become cantankerous and often belligerent. But he and I had several things in common.

Like me, Mr. Chase had worked for Fairchild Publications, selling advertising space. In addition, like my father, Mr. Chase had served in the army as an interpreter during World War II. He spoke Russian and claimed to be descended from Russian nobility. In fact, each year the *PennySaver's* Yorktown Printing division produced programs (gratis) for Tatiana, organizer of a black-tie ball for Russian aristocrats.

Mr. Chase enjoyed talking to me. He'd wander into my tiny office, sit in the lone guest chair, and recount stories from early years of the *PennySaver*.

I don't remember most of his reminiscences; I wish I had transcribed them all. But I did write down the following two stories.

PennySaver Competition

When Mr. Chase started the *PennySaver*, he was the only salesman, selling ads for his shopper in many towns in northern Westchester and Putnam counties including Yorktown, Somers, Mahopac, Carmel, Brewster, and Croton. Eventually it became too time-consuming for him to collect all the ads so he hired a man to pick up the ads he had already sold.

After a while, the "pick-up" man told Mr. Chase he was leaving to work for the publisher of the *Pleasantville Reminder* because that man was giving him a dollar raise.

"I didn't know you needed more money," Mr. Chase told him. "If you would have asked me, I would have given you a dollar raise. In fact, I'll give you the raise."

But the man said he had made a bargain to work for the other publisher and left.

What the man hadn't told Mr. Chase was that the other publisher wanted to start a competing Mahopac *PennySaver* and thought he was hiring Mr. Chase's salesman. The publisher didn't know his new employee's job was picking up already-sold ads.

As a result, the competing Mahopac *PennySaver* only published a one-page issue one week. And the "salesman" was fired after two weeks.

P.S. When *The Reminder* went out of business, Mr. Chase moved into Pleasantville with his *PennySaver*.

The Three Tommy Printers

When I worked for the *PennySaver*, the company had its own in-house printing operation, which we called "the shop." However, when Mr. Chase started his business, he used an outside printer. His first printer was Tommy from Mahopac, who raised prices whenever he felt like it.

Eventually Mr. Chase found another printer, Tommy from Peekskill, but this Tommy's print quality was poor.

Tommy from Mahopac asked Mr. Chase to return to him.

"Only if you sign a contract for a specific price so you can't change the price at will," Mr. Chase said.

Tommy from Mahopac agreed and the two of them worked out a contract. After Mr. Chase signed it, he asked Tommy from Mahopac for his signed copy.

"I'll sign it," Tommy promised. But he never did.

What Tommy from Mahopac did do, however, was raise his prices again.

During this time, a real estate man approached Mr. Chase about an available piece of land for his company. Mr. Chase purchased the property to construct a building that would become the *PennySaver's* first home at 1767 Front Street in Yorktown.

The printer who worked for Tommy from Mahopac (also named Tommy) found out about the project and told Mr. Chase he'd like to work for him.

When the building was finished, Tommy the printer for Tommy from Mahopac became Mr. Chase's in-house printer.

Mr. Chase informed Tommy from Mahopac that he would no longer be using his printing services.

"But we have a contract!" Tommy complained.

"You never signed it!" Mr. Chase argued.

"I'll sign it now," Tommy said.

Mr. Chase left Tommy from Mahopac anyway and the man sued him for breach of contract.

Mr. Chase asked his lawyer for advice.

"Don't worry," the lawyer said. "You have his printer."

Mr. Chase lost the suit and had to pay Tommy from Mahopac for breach of contract.

But Mr. Chase had finally found a good printer—a Tommy who worked directly for him.

ROAD TRIPS

When I wrote stories for the *PennySaver* that required accompanying photographs, I needed a person who could operate a camera, someone skilled in the art of taking pictures. That person certainly wasn't me; it was Pat.

A freelance photographer for our weekly paper, the *North County News*, Pat willingly accompanied me throughout the Hudson Valley, mostly to photograph advertisers for testimonials.

I'd ask retailers questions about their businesses and how the *PennySaver* helped them. The headline in these full-page features would be something like, "I love the *PennySaver* because..." or "My *PennySaver* ads really work!"

It was a win-win situation: The profiled business got a free ad and the *PennySaver* got a glowing review.

Since I hate to drive and Pat loved driving, we traveled in Pat's old station wagon, the back of the car continuously clanging because it contained a large carton filled with her empty soda cans.

Pat would drive just about anywhere. Her only requirement was that we didn't cross the Hudson River because she was terrified of bridges.

Nevertheless, one day on a trek to an advertiser near Poughkeepsie, Pat made a wrong turn and we wound up on the Newburgh-Beacon Bridge. Gripping the wheel tightly, Pat drove slowly across the Hudson into Ulster County, muttering to herself over and over, "I can do this..."

Another time, I was creating a special section about the town of Croton and wanted a scenic shot of the Croton Gorge. However, I hadn't realized getting the picture required the car to be perched on a ledge above the dam. That's when I discovered that in addition to being afraid of bridges, Pat was terrified of heights.

"No! No! No! No!" she shouted as she backed the car from the precarious ledge to more comfortable low-level ground— and I never did get a photo looking down into the gorge.

But except for those minor quirks, Pat was great—and so were her photos.

READY, AIM—FIRE?

As promotion manager for the *PennySaver*, I had the freedom to do many fun things — like create contests. Two of my favorite and most successful were *PennySaver* Prophet and Find the Phony Ad. But they were also the contests that nearly got me fired.

Both incidents occurred long ago and at the time, I didn't think they were at all funny. But in retrospect, the events seem kind of humorous. Here's what happened:

In January, 1991 the *PennySaver* moved from a cramped, long and narrow building at 1761 Front Street into a new facility at the end of the block. Since we were a seven-day operation (offices were open Monday through Friday and the shoppers were assembled Saturday and printed on Sunday), there was no good time to move.

But the time chosen was the worst for many of us: late Friday afternoon — our sales and editorial deadlines. So before moving, I had to pack up my many papers and materials, plus finish my weekly work.

That work included a new *PennySaver* Prophet contest. For each biweekly contest, I asked readers to make a prediction about something: a song, product, book, etc. For most of the 362 *PennySaver* Prophets, an artist created an accompanying cartoon, which I reviewed before publication.

However, on that crazy Friday evening, my cartoonist was also busy relocating to our new building so I asked Bob, the art director, to assign another artist to create a cartoon for Contest #59: SEQUEL SEARCH.

Contest #59 was a typical *PennySaver* Prophet. After mentioning current movie sequels (*Godfather III* and *Look Who's Talking Too*) and giving examples of possible sequels (*Grade School Cop* for *Kindergarten Cop* and *Misery Loves Company* for *Misery*), I asked readers to predict the next movie sequel.

When I finished moving into my new office, it was late and the art department was still working in the old building so I went home without seeing the accompanying *PennySaver* Prophet cartoon.

On Saturday morning, I got a phone call from the layout supervisor. Joyce had seen the cartoon in *PennySaver* Prophet and shown it to our boss, Mr. Chase.

"He had a fit," she told me.

"What was the cartoon?" I asked.

"You don't want to know," Joyce said, explaining she'd removed the artist's drawing and substituted an innocuous picture of Henry the Eighth.

When I returned to work on Monday, Joyce showed me the discarded cartoon. The artist had written "RETRO-SEQUEL: THE NEXT TO LAST TEMPTATION OF CHRIST" above a drawing of Jesus pointing to his tent and saying (in a word balloon) to two laughing men: "ALRIGHT, WHO'S THE SCHLEMIEL WHO PUT VANNA WHITE IN MY TENT?"

I was horrified at the mockery of religion, something the *PennySaver* never did. When I confronted Bob, he apologized for not having checked the artist's cartoon because he'd been so busy moving.

Later that morning, Bob and I were called into Mr. Chase's office together. After yelling at us for allowing the cartoon to almost appear in print, our boss threatened to fire both of us if something like that ever happened again. Mr. Chase had already fired the artist who had drawn the offensive cartoon.

But he wasn't upset with the cartoon's assault on religion. He was afraid Vanna White would sue the *PennySaver*.

———

Later that same year, I introduced the "Find the Phony Ad" contest to encourage people to read through *PennySaver* classified ads. Each week, a bogus classified ad would be mixed among the reader ads. People had to find the phony ad, mail it to us, and we'd choose a random winner.

Because the first contest coincided with Columbus Day, I created this holiday-themed debut ad:

> SAILORS NEEDED: Planning important ocean voyage to find new trade route to India. Need experienced sailors for 3 ships. Call New World Enterprises at 800-USA-1492. Ask for Chris C.

I thought my ad was quite clever. However, while I was congratulating myself, I forgot to do one important thing: Check the phone number.

By the time I discovered my bogus phone number was a legitimate exchange that belonged to a real estate company in Pennsylvania, it was too late. During the Columbus holiday week of 1991, the Pennsylvania firm received nearly a thousand phone calls from curious *PennySaver* readers.

And if that wasn't bad enough, our closest competitor, *The Reporter Dispatch*, a Westchester daily newspaper, found out about my mistake, interviewed someone in the real estate office about the annoying phone calls—and ran a huge front-page story insulting the *PennySaver*.

I was mortified. Hoping Mr. Chase, who preferred reading the *New York Times*, hadn't seen the newspaper article, I went to our comptroller to confess, apologize, and beg for my job. Fortunately, she was very understanding, told me not to worry, and assured me she would handle the boss.

I promised to make sure phone numbers in future phony ads would be non-working numbers. And true to my word, the contest ran 399 more times—without another misstep.

AUTHOR! AUTHOR!

BARNES & NOBLE STORE-Y

My first book-signing event after the publication of *DUST* in April of 2009 was with a group of independent authors at the nearby Barnes & Noble in Cortlandt Manor in July. Jennifer, the store's CRM (Customer Relations Manager) who organized the event, even baked chocolate chip cookies for us.

Jennifer gave each author a table and a freestanding sign (with name, book title, and cover picture) and positioned us along the left front wall, facing the registers. The setup was great because I could see a customer take my book to the checkout counter and pay for it.

That first book signing was a huge success. I sold lots of books and met several authors who became friends and future event partners.

But Barnes & Noble didn't run their events for free. They divided sales 60/40, with authors getting the larger percentage. However, not long after my initial event, Barnes & Noble changed the sales split so the store received the 60 percent share, greatly reducing the author's profit. In fact, one participant told me she lost 25 cents on every sale.

Also, in subsequent events, Barnes & Noble relocated independent authors to the center of the store, far from the registers. As a result, after that glorious beginning, I never sold many books there. And I too lost money—just in a different way.

Before doing signing events, I read suggestions about methods for increasing sales. "Let the customer hold your book," several gurus recommended, promising that tactic would help potential customers feel more attached to the book.

I thought the approach was worth a try so at an early Barnes & Noble event, I let a young woman with a nose ring hold a copy of *DUST* while she wandered through the store. Several minutes later, I watched nose ring-girl avoid the cash registers and walk out the door still carrying my book. That was the last time I used the "hold your book" approach.

A few years later, Barnes & Noble eliminated their CRMs and basically discontinued indy author book-signing events. But I was okay with that because by then I had found other, more profitable, venues.

Working with fellow independent authors, I lined up local vendor events—and for most venues we only had to split a small sign-up fee. I do most events with Linda Griffin, author of the children's books, *Adopting Ginger* and *Demetrius Says "No"* and the parenting book, *My Child Won't Listen...and other early childhood problems*, and my husband, Larry Berliner, author of the award-winning humor book, *You Can't Be Serious: An inner-city teacher a-muses about school and life*.

We call our joint signings YIKES! & TYKES & YUKS.

LOCATION! LOCATION! LOCATION!

Never doubt the importance of location—especially if you're selling books. It was crucial for the success of my first book signing at Barnes & Noble and it's been a factor in most of my events. Here are two notable examples:

For the Yorktown Grange Fair in July of 2010, my local Barnes & Noble graciously allocated a table for *DUST* next to the store's booth inside the main tent. But no one bought a book. In fact, hardly anyone stopped at my table. The only time people looked at the novel or flyers was when they were forced to stand next to my display during the neighboring cooking demonstration as they waited for a free taste of corn chowder.

And it wasn't just me. A former town supervisor who had occupied the same table earlier with her nonfiction books told me she too had no success.

After about an hour, my table was moved to the center of the tent—alone in the main aisle—because an exhibitor had paid for the space next to Barnes & Noble. The new location seemed good because people had to walk past my table. But again, everyone ignored me.

Finally, the nice folks at Barnes & Noble said I could stand inside their booth—and immediately everything changed. People looked at *DUST*, asked about it, and bought the novel. I didn't do anything differently. Only the location had changed.

———

The Brooklyn Book Festival, held each September in Brooklyn, NY, is, not surprisingly, a great place to sell books. But it's a huge event and much of an exhibitor's success depends on location, which is assigned randomly.

In 2011, I shared a booth at the event with Doris, a fellow independent novelist. However, the booth was expensive and we had to discount our books because of the heavy competition. The result: We both lost money.

But one good thing did happen that day in Brooklyn. At a nearby booth, we found Olive, owner of a small Yorktown company called DeMarche Publishing, who offered to carry our novels on consignment.

Olive took our books to out-of-state events, sold a few, and invited Doris and me to return to the Brooklyn Book Festival the next year to autograph our novels at DeMarche's booth. We thought that was much better (and cheaper!) than paying for our own booth so in September of 2012, Doris drove us back to Brooklyn.

At the Festival, we were amazed at DeMarche's location: It was the second booth inside the entrance—and the first booth was empty.

After an hour, during which Doris and I each sold some books, we realized that the first booth, which the sign said belonged to a men's magazine, was still vacant. We decided to "borrow" the booth until it was claimed.

So that's what we did. Grabbing our books and bookmarks (we didn't have posters or a tablecloth because we hadn't expected to have our own space), we stood behind the bare first table and sold lots of novels—until the men's magazine people showed up.

The following year, Olive again invited Doris and me to Brooklyn to sign our books at her company's table. But this time, DeMarche had a horrible location: The booth was on the outside perimeter of the Festival, the sidewalk adjoining the street. As a result, many of the people who strolled past weren't even visiting the Brooklyn Book Festival. Not surprisingly, I sold very few books.

It's all about location.

THE GOOD, THE BAD, AND THE UGLY

It's easy to evaluate book signings: If you sell lots of books, it's a good signing and if you don't sell lots of books, it's a bad signing.

An ugly signing? That's when really bad things happen and I've also had one of those. Here's a recap:

The Good

I've recounted some of these events already: My first book signing [see "Barnes & Noble Store-y," p. 163] and the incidents depicted in "Location! Location! Location!" [p. 165] were successful mostly because of their locations.

But I've also had good book signings in unusual places, like JV Hot Bagels in Jefferson Valley, NY. The secret to my success there was "online" sales: As the crowd waited on line outside to enter the store, they had nothing to do but read my bookmarks—and plenty of time to buy my books.

———

I've done well at YIKES! & TYKES events in schools with children's and parenting book author, Linda Griffin. At Buchanan-Verplanck Elementary School in Buchanan (October,

2015), I read stories from *The Sea Crystal and Other Weird Tales* to third, fourth, and fifth graders. Similarly, at St. Patrick's School in Yorktown (February, 2020), I read my stories to students in grades three through eight. Afterwards at both school events, Linda and I sold copies of our books to children, parents, and teachers.

————

The best time of year for signings is November through early December when everyone is shopping for presents—and autographed books make great gifts.

I've had successful signings in small venues. Although the holiday fair at the Asbury United Methodist Church in Croton had just twenty tables crowded into the church's basement, the event was well-advertised, well-attended—and visitors bought books.

I've also had successful church functions in larger locations. Holy Rosary Church's fair in Thornwood includes as many as seventy tables inside the parish school's gym. (Churches with adjoining schools are great venues because organizers can use students to publicize the event.) Our secret again was location: YIKES! & TYKES & YUKS (me, Linda Griffin, and Larry Berliner) has always had a table at the front entrance.

————

My best book signing didn't occur during the holiday season. In March of 2015, Linda Griffin and I participated in Main Street Market, held in the lower level of the Westchester County Center in White Plains.

At the same time, another event—the Home Show—was happening upstairs in the main level. And the Home Show was huge, well advertised, and charged an admissions fee—a really good thing: It meant attendees had money they were willing to spend.

But our Main Street Market vendors also had attractions for shoppers. In addition to books, we offered unique items like local wines, handcrafted pens, and food (homemade pickles, chocolate balls, and stuffed cabbage). We featured entertainment too—a terrific guitar-playing duo crooned ballads and Beatles' tunes.

The event included one other plus: Our coordinators went up to the Home Show and ushered people downstairs to our food and crafts tables, giving us lots of traffic.

I sold many books that day (two customers bought all of mine) and Linda and I planned to participate in more of these five-times-a-year events. But that didn't happen. Sadly, Main Street Market was cancelled after the March event.

––––––

Ferry Festa, which I participated in with Westchester Indie Authors in October of 2016, was held outside on Main Street in Dobbs Ferry. It was my longest fair, running from 1 pm to 8 pm.

It was also my most lucrative event. A children's book editor who bought *The Sea Crystal and Other Weird Tales* at Ferry Festa, loved my short stories so much, she hired me to create tales for a major educational publisher. I made more money writing two stories for sixth graders than I've earned in all my years of selling books at signing events.

The Bad

I've had signings where I haven't sold any books. Sometimes it was because not enough people attended the event, due to lack of publicity or a poor location. If there's no traffic, it's hard to sell anything. And other times, some vendors sold items and I didn't. That's not fun, but it happens.

For a few fairs, I've been assigned a bad location and then moved to a more trafficked area. That's been the case in several mall events.

It also occurred at a Halloween Festival and Parade in Mesier Park in Wappingers Falls in October of 2019. YIKES! & TYKES & YUKS was given a space on a side path next to only one other vendor (a witch selling broomsticks) and when the costumed children and parents started parading, it was along the main path where they didn't pass—or even see—our table. After getting permission, we moved our table (with help) along the parade route and I sold a few books.

The Ugly

In June of 2019, I was a vendor at the local Elks Club in Yorktown, an event that had many issues. First, we had the problem of location. Although this venue was near a main road, the building was hidden so most people (even local residents) had no idea it was there. I had suggested posting large signs and balloons at the main intersection, but the organizers just put up tiny signs and a few little balloons.

Traffic? We had practically none. I didn't even give away a bookmark and nearly all sales were vendor to vendor.

Here's the ugly part: In the middle of the afternoon, one of the event coordinators, who had been drinking at the bar, got into a shouting match with a vendor (actually the event coordinator did all the shouting). The woman was so loud and her language was so obscene—bringing the attacked vendor's child to tears—that the police were called.

Now that's the definition of an ugly event.

WEIRD THINGS REALLY DO HAPPEN

Since I write supernatural thrillers, people sometimes ask me if I've ever had an out-of-this-world experience. My answer is "yes." Twice. Both occurred during book-signing events.

The first weird happening took place at the Tazza Café in Somers in June of 2010. When I arrived for the signing event that morning, I discovered the electricity had suddenly gone off moments before.

When did the power come back on? The café owner escorted me to the restroom several hours later and just as I flicked on the light switch—forgetting we had no power—the electricity returned.

That experience gave both of us goose bumps. "Do you have paranormal abilities?" the man asked.

It was an interesting question. Could writing *DUST* have given me some kind of supernatural talent?

Apparently not. According to news reports, heavy winds had knocked down a nearby power line. So much for my new career as Electric Woman.

———

The second weird happening was at a book signing at Bethel, a facility for seniors in Ossining in September of 2012. Although it was a rainy day, the event was held outdoors. As a result, Linda Griffin and I had to display our books under a protected porch.

Then, a few minutes before noon, we heard a siren blast. After looking for the source of the noise, we discovered it was coming from Linda's phone.

The siren turned out to be a tornado warning, instructing us to "Seek shelter indoors immediately!" So after quickly packing up our books and signs, we moved into the building's lobby.

Several residents of Bethel joined us. One woman, who was 100-years-old, asked to see my novels and then purchased *DUST*, a thriller about an evil dust devil—a miniature tornado.

So I sold a book about a whirlwind to a 100-year-old lady during a tornado warning. And that woman's name? It was Dorothy. *Wizard of Oz*, anyone?

Susan Berliner has always been a writer. But this book is different: It's not a supernatural thriller. It's not a collection of weird short stories. It's about Susan.

Entertaining long-ago journal entries (*Diary of a Young Reporter*) partner with oodles of quirky short takes like these:

* attending a Hasidic bar mitzvah (*The Goyisher Table*)
* floundering at the bottom of the alphabet (*Growing Up "W"*)
* socializing at a college houseplan party (*When Susan Met Harriet*)
* nearly losing her job—twice (*Ready, Aim—Fire?*)
* book signing escapades (*The Good, the Bad, and the Ugly*)

Got a few minutes? Enjoy an episode from Susan Berliner's life.

SUSAN BERLINER is the author of six supernatural thrillers and two collections of short stories. She has worked as a newspaper reporter, editor, promotion manager, and nonfiction writer. Susan lives with her husband, Larry, in Yorktown Heights, New York.

ISBN 978-1-7374163-0-2

Check out her fiction at **susanberliner.com**